MW00438573

REVELATIONS AND VISIONS

Revelations and Visions

*Discerning the
True and the Certain
from the False or the Doubtful*

Augustin Poulain, SJ

Translated by Leonora L. Yorke Smith

Edited and with an Introduction by
Bro. Frank Sadowski, SSP

ALBA·HOUSE   NEW·YORK

SOCIETY OF ST. PAUL, 2187 VICTORY BLVD., STATEN ISLAND, NEW YORK 10314

ST PAULS

Library of Congress Cataloging-in-Publication Data

Poulain, Aug. (Augustin), 1836-1919.
   [Des grâces d'oraison. Part 4. English]
   Revelations and visions: discerning the true and the certain from the
false or the doubtful / Augustin Poulain; translated by Leonora L. Yorke
Smith; edited and with an introduction by Frank Sadowski.
     p.   cm.
   Includes bibliographical references.
   ISBN 0-8189-0793-2
   1. Private revelations. 2. Visions.   I. Sadowski, Frank.
II. Title.
BV5091.R4P6813   1998
248.2'9—dc21   97-207419
                                  CIP

Produced and designed in the United States of America by the
Fathers and Brothers of the Society of St. Paul,
2187 Victory Boulevard, Staten Island, New York 10314,
as part of their communications apostolate.

ISBN: 0-8189-0793-2

© Copyright 1998 by the Society of St. Paul

Printing Information:

Current Printing - first digit	1	2	3	4	5	6	7	8	9	10

Year of Current Printing - first year shown

1998	1999	2000	2001	2002	2003	2004	2005

TABLE OF CONTENTS

INTRODUCTION
BRO. FRANK SADOWSKI, SSP

Revelations and Visions in Today's Context

This book, *Revelations and Visions*, is a reprint of Part IV (chapters XX-XXIII) of *The Graces of Interior Prayer*, by Augustin Poulain, S.J. The book was originally published in France in 1901 under the title *Des Grâces D'Oraison*. The English-language edition of the book was translated by Leonora L. Yorke Smith and was published in 1910.

The Graces of Interior Prayer is a formidable tome about 650 pages long. If I had ever seen it on a library shelf, I would have passed it by as a dry, outdated treatise, most likely a sort of longer and duller version of Tanquerey's *The Spiritual Life*.

Some years ago, a confrere recommended *The Graces of Interior Prayer* to me for its discussion of private revelations and visions. To my surprise, I found that it was a practical, readable work, firmly based on the insights of St. John of the Cross and St. Teresa of Avila. I thought it was a shame that this material was not more accessible to a wider audience. Now, at last, it is; I hope it will be useful for pastors, spiritual directors, and anyone wishing to learn more about the subject.

Father Poulain, of course, did not have the final word on private revelations and visions. The century following the publication of his book has seen great advances in our understanding of psychology, neuroscience, spiritual direction and mysticism. These limitations, however, are incidental. The reader will find Father

Poulain a dependable guide who relies on the Doctors of the Church as well as his own common sense and experience. His book, as we will see, received the approbation of Pope St. Pius X.

Such a guide is certainly necessary today. The world is flooded with Catholic and non-Catholic seers, visionaries, prophets, and the like. How do you discern the true from the false? How do you give spiritual direction to a visionary? How (if necessary) do you defend yourself (or your parish, or your religious community) from them?

The reader will see that in these matters not much has changed in the last century. There is very little that can be said (for example) about Maria Valtorta's *The Poem of the Man-God* that Father Poulain has not said here about the writings of Anne Catherine Emmerich and Mary of Agreda.

But who was Father Poulain? And how did he come to write this book? Let's see.

The Life and Writings of Father Augustin Poulain

Augustin François Poulain was born in 1836 in Cherbourg, France. He entered the Jesuit novitiate in 1858 and pronounced his final vows in 1877. Among his many offices, he was a professor of mathematics, the director of an artist's guild, and a librarian. He lived in Paris from 1898 until his death in 1919.

In the words of J.V. Bainvel, who wrote a biographical sketch of him for *The Graces of Interior Prayer*, Father Poulain "was naturally of a witty and happy disposition and diffused gladness all around him; the clearness of his mind is manifest in all he wrote." He even brought this witty approach to a *Treatise on Geometry* that he wrote: "He used in fun to call this work the 'Poor Man's Geometry,' for he had devoted all his ingenious and inventive wit to simplifying the theorems so as to bring them within the reach of the meanest intellect."

At first glance, it may seem surprising that a man with this background wrote an outstanding study of mysticism, *The Graces of Interior Prayer*. In fact, Father Poulain had a serious and long-standing interest in the subject, based on study, personal experience, and his work as a spiritual director.

Bainvel tells us: "In spite of his jealous care never to open his soul to profane eyes, it may be guessed that he had himself felt the mystical touch. Once at least he confided in a young religious capable of understanding him that his mystical experience had gone as far as the prayer of quiet, no farther." Father Poulain, then, was writing from personal experience when he stated: "Instead of feeling a certain pride because we have arrived at the prayer of quiet, we ought to ask ourselves fearfully why we have not gone beyond it."

The Graces of Interior Prayer is also enlivened by Father Poulain's work as a spiritual director. In 1901 he wrote: "In thirty years I have come to know 33 persons who seem to have real supernatural graces, and nine who have false visions." He also wrote: "In the absence of other qualities, this book will, I think, possess that of being a conscientious piece of work. For the last forty years I have studied these questions steadily in view of it. I have read quantities of treatises, ranging from duodecimos to folios. I have interrogated at great length numbers of persons possessing the graces of interior prayer, and others who were under the illusion that this was so in their case also. An acquaintance with these last is also useful. If the reader detects any error, or finds me too obscure, I beg him to tell me so quite frankly. I am not afraid of objections and contradictions. They have almost always taught me something, if it were only that I could make some distinction clearer."

Father Poulain kept this promise in the improvements he made in later editions of *The Graces of Interior Prayer*. In Bainvel's words: "The author was careful to profit by everything: criticisms, the questions which were put to him from all directions, new experiences, contact with a larger number of souls, the growing number of publications and courses of lectures, both on mysticism and on kindred questions (lives of the saints or pious persons, studies of experimental psychology or pathology, rationalist schemes and explanations or the replies of Christian apologists); he managed to

bring all these within his wide and elastic framework, like a collec-
tor labelling, classifying and enriching his collection."

Although Father Poulain wrote a book on *The Mysticism of
St. John of the Cross* in 1893, and wrote elsewhere on mysticism (for
example, he wrote the articles "Contemplation" and "Revelations,
Private" for *The Catholic Encyclopedia*, first published in 1912), *The
Graces of Interior Prayer* remains in a class by itself.

In the first twenty years after its publication, *The Graces of
Interior Prayer* went through nine editions, with a sale of some
20,000 copies. By 1914, it had been translated into English, German, Italian and Spanish.

In the decades preceding Vatican II, countless priests were
exposed to Father Poulain's ideas through Adolphe Tanquerey's *The
Spiritual Life: A Treatise on Ascetical and Mystical Theology*, a standard seminary textbook which went through many printings. It was
translated into English in 1932. Its section on private revelations,
for example, not only directly cites *The Graces of Interior Prayer*
several times, but also uses many of the same examples of false visions, incorrect prophecies, etc.

More recently, Fr. Benedict J. Groeschel, C.F.R., frequently
cited Father Poulain in his 1993 book, *A Still, Small, Voice: A Practical Guide on Reported Revelations*. He writes: "I have drawn much
from the standard work, *The Graces of Interior Prayer* by Father
Augustin Poulain, S.J.… Anyone more seriously interested in alleged private revelations must study this great work…" (pp. 12-13).

In 1904, Father Poulain received a letter of warm praise for
his book from Cardinal Steinhuber, the Prefect of the Sacred Congregation of the Index. This was followed in 1907 by a letter of
approbation from Pope Pius X. They read as follows:

[*Translation*]

Letter from His Eminence, Cardinal Steinhuber,
Prefect of the Sacred Congregation of the Index
(Respecting the First Edition).

Reverend Father,

It is with real satisfaction that I have read your Reverence's book on *Des Grâces d'Oraison*. I cannot resist the desire to congratulate you with all my heart upon this fine and useful work. Directors of souls and the masters of the spiritual life will draw from it abundant supplies of enlightenment and the counsels necessary to enable them to solve the many complicated questions that they will encounter. What pleases me is the simplicity, the clearness, and the precision of your exposition, and still more the solidity of the teaching. I can say the same for the care that you have taken to rely upon the old and approved masters who have written on the subject of mysticism. You dispel their obscurities, you reconcile their apparent contradictions, and you give their language the turn that the spirit and the speech of modern times demand. I pray God ardently to bless the labour that you have undergone in order to aid and console so many souls. May He assure an ever-increasing circulation to your book.

I salute you in Our Lord.

Your devoted servant in Christ,
✠ A. Cardinal Steinhuber
Rome, March 16, 1904

APPROBATION OF HIS HOLINESS POPE PIUS X
(FOR THE FIFTH EDITION)

———————————————

[*Translation*]

Reverend Father,

The Holy Father has confided to me the agreeable mission of conveying to you his warm and sincere thanks for the remarkable treatise on Mystical Theology entitled: *Des Grâces d'Oraison*, the fifth edition of which you have just published. His Holiness is rejoiced at the fruitful result of your long years of study, spent in observing the ways of grace in souls aspiring to perfection. He is happy to see that now, thanks to you, directors of consciences possess a work of great worth and high utility. You not only rely upon the incontestable doctrine of the old masters who have treated this very difficult subject, but you present these teachings, which constitute your authorities, under the form that our age requires. While wishing your work a great success and abundant spiritual fruits, His Holiness grants to your Paternity the Apostolic Benediction.

In acquainting you with this favour, I am happy to assure you of the sentiments of high esteem with which I am,

Yours very affectionately in the Lord,
✠ Cardinal Merry Del Val
Rome, April 2, 1907

FOR FURTHER READING

There is a vast and ever-growing body of literature about St. John of the Cross and St. Teresa of Avila, as well as various editions and translations of their writings. I recommend the editions from ICS Publications: *The Collected Works of St. John of the Cross* (1964, 1973, 1991) and *The Collected Works of St. Teresa of Avila* (3 volumes: 1976, 1980, 1985). The Classics of Western Spirituality series of Paulist Press includes convenient editions of many of the visionary saints mentioned by Father Poulain, such as Angela of Foligno, Birgitta of Sweden, Catherine of Genoa, Catherine of Siena, Hildegard of Bingen, Ignatius of Loyola, John of the Cross, and Teresa of Avila.

The following are some books that I found useful and interesting. Woodward and Zimdars-Swartz have good bibliographies for those wishing to further study private visions, revelations, and related phenomena.

Norman Cohn. *The Pursuit of the Millennium* (Oxford University Press, 1957, 1970). A terrifying picture of the lunatic visionaries who infested medieval Europe. Some of them were uncannily similar to the Charles Manson gang and the Heaven's Gate cult.

R.G. Culleton. *The Prophets and Our Times* and *The Reign of Antichrist* (TAN Books, both titles 1974). These two books are invaluable compilations of Catholic private revelations and prophecies.

Anne Catherine Emmerich. *The Dolorous Passion of Our Lord Jesus Christ* (1983), *The Life of Jesus Christ & Biblical Revelations* (4 volumes, 1986), *The Life of the Blessed Virgin Mary* (1970). All titles, TAN Books.

Hilda Graef. *Mary: A History of Doctrine and Devotion* (Sheed and Ward, 2 volumes, 1963, 1965; reprinted in one volume by

Christian Classics, 1985). Contains a good account of Marian apparitions, as well as of some unusual and excessive devotional practices.

Benedict J. Groeschel. *A Still, Small, Voice: A Practical Guide to Reported Revelations* (Ignatius Press, 1993). As already mentioned, this book draws on *The Graces of Interior Prayer* quite extensively. It is a sound guide, written for a general audience.

Ronald A. Knox. *Enthusiasm: A Chapter in the History of Religion* (Oxford University Press, 1950; University of Notre Dame Press, 1994). A classical study of aberrant spirituality.

Mary of Agreda. *Mystical City of God* (4 volumes, AMI Press, 1971); *Mystical City of God*, abridged edition (TAN Books, 1978 and AMI Press, 1981).

Karl Rahner. *Visions and Prophecies* (Burns and Oates, 1963; also in *Inquiries*, Herder and Herder, 1964, pp. 87-188). A classic study, with many startling examples.

Carl E. Schmoger. *Life of Anne Catherine Emmerich* (2 volumes, TAN Books, 1976).

Kenneth L. Woodward. *Making Saints* (Simon and Schuster, 1990, 1991). An invaluable book. In the context of the processes of beatification and canonization, it examines several aspects of private revelations and visions, as well as stigmata and other unusual phenomena. Among many other things of interest, it has a good account of the attempts to have Anne Catherine Emmerich beatified.

Sandra L. Zimdars-Swartz. *Encountering Mary: From La Salette to Medjugorje* (Princeton University Press, 1991; Avon Books, 1992). An outstanding book that provides a detailed, objective, accurate and well-researched account of the Marian apparitions of the last century and a half.

A Word about the Text and Notes

I have edited Father Poulain's text very conservatively, for the most part confining myself to bringing spellings into line with American usage, correcting a few misprints, and in a few cases changing hopelessly obsolete words. The chapter notes are by Father Poulain. At the end of the book, I have added some historical and biographical notes, covering the (mostly obscure) authors cited in the text, as well as a number of historical events more familiar to a French audience than to an American one. In writing these notes, I used *The Graces of Interior Prayer* and the old edition of *The Catholic Encyclopedia*.

REVELATIONS AND VISIONS

CHAPTER ONE

DESCRIPTIVE PART

1. — From the point of view of sanctification, these graces are of much **less importance** than is mystic union.

Many Christians think otherwise. They are misled by the preponderance given to revelations in the majority of the *Lives* of the saints. They imagine that these graces occupied as large a place in the saint's existence as in the accounts of their lives.

The compilers of these books have been led to treat facts in this way because the mystic union is so simple and intangible that ten lines have often contained all that a saint has been able to say on the subject, while visions lend themselves to long narrations. Also the writer understands them better. And, finally, he knows that by appealing to their imagination he will please his readers more.

1. Various kinds of revelations

2. — There are **three kinds** of supernatural **locutions**, or words, corresponding in order of superiority to the faculties that come into play: the bodily hearing, the imagination, and the intelligence.

3. — 1° The **exterior** or *auricular* **locutions** are heard by the ear, as is the case with natural speech. Sounds are received, but they are produced supernaturally.

4. — 2° Imaginative locutions[1] are also composed of words like the foregoing; but they are received directly without the assistance of the ear. They can be said to be received by the imaginative sense. They, with those that come after them, are included in the term interior locutions.

5. — 3° Intellectual locutions. This is a simple communication of thought without words, and consequently without the use of any definite language. "It is our Lord's will" (says St. Teresa) "... that the soul should have some knowledge of what passes in Heaven; and I think that, as the blessed there without speech understand one another... so it is here" (*Life*, ch. xxvii, 12).

The human mind itself sometimes dispenses with words. For when we are writing it often happens that we say: I cannot find words that express my thought exactly.

Both good and bad angels can speak to us intellectually, but on condition that God intervenes to give us, momentarily, at any rate, the faculty to understand them. Otherwise they can only, in this world, act upon our bodies or imaginations.

The same thing must be said with regard to intellectual visions of angels.

6. — St. John of the Cross makes use of an expression that I shall not employ, because it seems to me to be too obscure. He gives the name of intellectual **"successive locutions"** to speech that would be designated with greater clearness as apparent speech. It is that which is produced by the mind, either by its own activity alone or with a real foundation, defining and *arranging* certain truths that God has revealed to us or other seeming truths presented to us by the Devil. In reality, God says nothing, but this is how the illusion arises: In certain cases the mind "puts words and reasonings together so much to the purpose, and with such facility and clearness, that it discovers by reflection things it knew not before [or that it had forgotten], in such a way that it seems to itself as if it was not itself which did so, but some third person which addressed it interiorly, reasoning, answering, and informing.... Thus the mind addresses itself to itself as if to some other person" (*Ascent of Mount Carmel,* ch. xxix, p. 189).

Since these are not true words, I prefer to designate them accordingly. And, further, the word *successive* suggests that the true intellectual words never deserve this name. Now, the saint says the contrary in the following chapter. "Sometimes it is one word, at another two or more, and occasionally *successive words,* as in the former case; for they continue in the way of instruction to the soul" (*ibid.,* ch. xxx, p. 196).

See in No. **25** two other expressions employed by the saint.

7. — The **visions** also are of **three kinds**.

8. — 1° **Exterior visions**, also called *ocular* and *corporeal*,[2] are visions perceived by the bodily eyes. A material being is formed, or seems to be formed, outside of us, and we perceive it like anything else that is round about us.

9. — 2° **Imaginative visions** are visions of material objects, seen without the assistance of the eyes. They are perceived by the imaginative sense.

10. — 3° **Intellectual visions** are visions perceived by the mind alone without any interior image. We may thus see God or the angels, and even material objects, but in the same way as one would see angels intellectually, without any form, that is to say. These visions may be either confused or distinct (see Extracts, **49**).

11. — The visions that occur during **ecstasy** or in a dream, belong (save in the case of a miraculous exception) to one of the two last categories, for, normally, the action of the eyes is suspended during the ecstasy.

Some of the states that the Holy Scriptures call prophetic sleep may perhaps in reality have been ecstasies.

12. — When either good or evil **angels** appear in a corporeal or imaginative vision, what we see is not really them, because they have no bodies. It is a borrowed form. In much the same way, when we see another person, we do not really see his or her soul in that person's face.

When the Devil appears under a bodily form, there is nothing to prevent him from giving himself the same charm, the same air of holiness, as a good angel. If the vision is intellectual, the mask falls off, except perhaps when the vision is very obscure.

St. Bridget says that if we were to see an angel quite clearly we should die of pleasure, and that if it were a demon we should die with fright and horror (Book II, ch. xviii).

13. — It is possible also to have an **intellectual view of our own soul**. In the natural state we are conscious only of our mental activities, and we thence *conclude* the existence of our faculties. But God can raise us supernaturally to a higher knowledge, and show us our nature such as it actually is, and can even cause us to see our state of grace, etc. In Heaven we shall have all these kinds of knowledge.

14. — St. Alphonsus Liguori truly remarks that "the revelations of secret or of future things, such as the mysteries of the Faith, the reading of consciences, the predestination of certain persons, their death, their elevation to some dignity, and other similar things, may occur in three ways: by visions, by locutions, and by a simple apprehending of the truth" (*Homo apost.*, Appendix I, No. 22).

15. — History proves that visions or exterior locutions have often been received, transiently, at any rate, by persons who were still in the way of ordinary prayer. The apparition to the children at La Salette would seem to be a case of this kind. But visions and supernatural locutions of a higher order are not *usually* granted, with any frequency, at least, until the **period of ecstasy** is almost reached.

St. Teresa of Avila heard words before she had visions. Here is a summary of her graces and the order in which she received them:

16. — **The progress of mystic graces with St. Teresa:**
1° At the age of twenty (1535) she passed a year in a state of

recollection and received the *prayer of quiet* or *full union* from time to time for "the space of an Ave Maria" on each occasion (*Life*, ch. iv, 9).

2° She afterwards relaxes in fervor, recovers it at the age of forty (1555), and is again favored with the *mystic union* (*Life*, ch. xxiii, 2). Two years later St. Francis Borgia reassures her with regard to her way of prayer (*Life*, ch. xxiv, 4). Some time before this she had made the Exercises of St. Ignatius under the direction of Fr. Juan de Padranos.

3° At the age of forty-three (1558) she places herself under the direction of Fr. Balthasar Alvarez, who was twenty-five years of age, and she had her first ecstasy while she was imploring Our Lord to set her free from certain too natural friendships, with regard to which her Confessor expostulated with her (*Life*, ch. xxiv, 6). She then begins to hear interior locutions (*Life*, ch. xxv), which raises a great storm against her. Her confessors order her to reject these locutions. She continues in a great agony of mind for two years. Her friends pray that she may be led by a way less open to suspicion. She tries vainly to desire this herself (*Life*, ch. xxvii).

4° About two years later, at the age of forty-five, she is favored with visions of Our Lord (*Life*, ch. xxvi, 6). These visions were at first intellectual (*Life*, ch. xxvii), and lasted continually for two years and a half[3] (*Life*, ch. xxix, 2). She saw Our Savior at her right hand and continually at her side, and walking with her[4] (*Life*, ch. xxvii, 3), and St. Peter and St. Paul on her left hand (*Life*, ch. xxix, 6). St. Peter of Alcantara reassured her with regard to these favors towards the year 1560, and he thus put an end to her anguish and her resistance to them (*Life*, ch. xxx, 5).

5° Some time after the first of these visions she had some *imaginative* visions. On the first occasion she saw Our Savior's Hands only (*Life*, ch. xxviii, 2); a few days later His divine Face; and finally she saw His whole Person. She saw Him almost always as He was after the Resurrection, in His glorified Body (*Life*, ch. xxix, 4). She never had any exterior visions (*Life*, ch. xxviii, 5; xxx, 5; *Interior Castle*, Sixth Mansion, ch. ix, 3), nor heard auricular words (*Relation* VII, 4, made for Fr. Rodrigo Alvarez, S.J., *Life*, p. 445). God the Father spoke to her at times, the Holy Spirit never, the Word very often, but always by means of His Sacred Humanity (*Relation* VIII, 20, 21, to Fr. Rodrigo Alvarez, *Life*, p. 463).

6° At the age of fifty-one (about 1566) she concludes the book of her *Life* and composes the *Way of Perfection*. After her raptures were over she was seized by a most grievous pain, the yearning to see God. "This is my present state.… It is a communication made, not to console, but to show the reason why the soul must be weary: because it is far away from the Good which in itself comprehends all good" (*Life*, ch. xx, 11, 12). "The sufferer gives vent to loud cries, which she cannot stifle… there is great danger of death in this state. Short as is the time during which it lasts [in its greatest intensity], it leaves the limbs all disjointed…" (*Interior Castle*, Sixth Mansion, ch. xi, 3, 4).

7° At the age of fifty-seven (the end of 1572) she is raised to the *spiritual marriage*. This was fourteen years after her first ecstasy and ten before her death. She died at the age of sixty-seven (1582). She had composed the *Interior Castle* five years earlier.

---

2. Descriptive details concerning interior locutions

---

17. — We shall occupy ourselves principally with *imaginative* words. I shall follow St. Teresa (*Life*, chs. xxv, xxvi, xxvii; *Interior Castle*, Sixth Mansion, chs. iii, iv). It is solely a question of true words.

18. — 1° **When do they occur?** Often outside the ecstasy; and then it is frequently unexpected and when the mind is occupied with other things. "It may occur, too, when the understanding and the soul are so troubled and distracted that they cannot form one sentence correctly" (*Life*, ch. xxv, 6).

So, too, when the locutions are intellectual it happens that "generally — so I think — the senses are not taken away, and the faculties are not suspended: they preserve their ordinary state" (*Life*, ch. xxvii, 9).

"… If we see *visions* and hear *words*, it never is as at the time when the soul is in union *in the very rapture itself*.… The soul is then wholly in the power of another… but when this instant is passed, the soul continuing still entranced, then is the time of which I am speaking; for the faculties, though not completely suspended, are so disposed that they are scarcely active, being, as it were, absorbed and incapable of making any reflections" (*Life*, ch. xxv, 7).

19. — 2° **Clarity.** The interior words "are very distinctly formed. . . they are, however, *much more clearly understood* than they would be if they were heard by the ear" (*Life*, ch. xxv, 2). "The divine locution is a voice so clear that not a syllable of its utterance is lost" (*ibid.*, 6). As a rule, the words that are counterfeited by the imagination are undecided, without consistency; the phrase hesitates and is left unfinished.

20. — 3° **Strength.** "…There is no escape, for, in spite of ourselves, we must listen; and the understanding must apply itself so thoroughly to the comprehension of that which God wills we should hear, that it is nothing to the purpose whether we will it or not. . . . My resistance lasted nearly two years [at the age of forty-two and forty-three] because of the great fear I was in: and even now I resist occasionally; but it is of no use" (*Life*, ch. xxv, 2). "The soul is like a person whose hearing was good, and who is not suffered to stop his ears, while people standing *close beside him* speak to him with *a loud voice.* He may be unwilling to hear, yet hear he must" (*Life*, ch. xxvii, 10). "Those Our Lord does not lead by this path may suppose that the soul can avoid listening to these locutions, and that even if they be interior it is at least possible to distract the mind from them, and so escape such dangers. This cannot be done" (*Interior Castle*, Sixth Mansion, ch. iii, 27).

21. — 4° **Certainty.** "*The words*, their effects, and the assurance they carried with them *convinced the soul at the moment* that they came from God. That time, however, is now past: doubts afterwards arise whether the locutions come from the Devil or from the imagination, although while hearing them, the person had no doubt of their truth, which she would have died to defend" (*Interior Castle*, Sixth Mansion, ch. iii, 12).

It is only afterwards that doubts may arise (*Life*, ch. xxv, 10).

22. — 5° What feelings, what emotional states, do these words produce? "The second sign is a great calm [after the first moment, that is to say], and a devout and peaceful recollection which dwell in the soul, together with a desire to praise God. . . . If these locutions proceed from the imagination, they show no such signs, bringing neither conviction, nor peace, nor interior joy with them.[5] ... But Satan could never counterfeit the effects spoken of; he leaves no peace nor light in the soul, only anxiety and confusion" (*Interior Castle*, Sixth Mansion, ch. iii, 10, 16, 24). The saint also speaks of "the great aridity which remains in the soul after these evil locutions... yet this disquiet is such that I know not whence it comes" (*Life*, ch. xxv, 13).

23. — 6° The majesty of these words. "As to the divine locution, we listen to that as we do to a person of great holiness, learning, or authority... for these locutions proceed occasionally in such great majesty that, without our recollecting who it is that utters them, they make us tremble if they be words of reproof, and die of love if words of love" (*Life*, ch. xxv, 9).

24. — 7° Instantaneous knowledge. "The divine locutions instruct us without loss of time, and we understand matters which seem to require a month on our part to arrange" (*Life*, ch. xxv, 12).[6] The meaning of these locutions is therefore fuller than that of our own words.

25. — 8° The effects upon the conduct. There is one case in which these are very evident; it is when the divine locutions counsel or command an *interior disposition*; for instance, if they bid the soul be at peace or correct some defect, they produce this change *suddenly* in the soul. "When Our Lord speaks, it is at once word and work" (*Life*, ch. xxv, 5), like the Word by which the world was created.

St. Teresa says that this is the most decisive test of all, as proving that a locution is from God. On the other hand, "the words formed by the understanding effect nothing" (*Life*, ch. xxv, 5; *Interior Castle*, Sixth Mansion, ch. iii).

Locutions of this nature might be styled *operative* locutions. St. John of the Cross applies the name *substantial* to them, which does not suggest clearly the work that they perform (*Ascent of Mount Carmel*, Book II, ch. xxxi, p. 200). "The soul is not called upon to do or attempt anything with regard to these locutions, but to be resigned and humble." He adds that neither the intellect nor the evil spirit can imitate this action (*ibid.*). This is easily understood, because the Devil cannot seek to produce a real transformation of the will, in a good sense; and the intellect cannot accomplish it without the help of some previous considerations.

The saint says that there exist, on the contrary, cases where, although the locutions are divine "and render it [the soul] ready to accomplish what is commanded" (*ibid.*, ch. xxx, p. 196), yet the effect on the mind is not great, which doubtless means that the efficacy depends upon our free-will, which may resist it.[7] He gives as an example the divine command that Moses received to go and speak to Pharaoh. Moses angered God by his resistance [cf. Exodus 4:13-14].

Words sent chiefly to enlighten the mind, such as prophetic warnings, or even commands to execute some exterior work, are generally of this number.

26. — 9° **Persistence in the memory.** "The third proof is that these words do not pass from the memory, but remain there for a very long time; *sometimes they are never forgotten*" (*Interior Castle*, Sixth Mansion, ch. iii, 11).

"The divine locution is a work done; and though some of it may be forgotten, and time have lapsed, yet it is not so wholly forgotten that the memory loses all traces of what was once spoken — unless, indeed, after a very long time, or unless the locution were words of grace or of instruction. But as to prophetic words, they are never forgotten in my opinion" (*Life*, ch. xxv, 10).

26 *bis*. — 10° **Whence do these locutions proceed?** "Sometimes," says Alvarez de Paz, "they seem to descend from the sky, sometimes to be uttered near by or at a distance, sometimes to rise up from the heart's profoundest depths" (*De Inquis. pacis*, Book V, Part III, ch. vi).[8]

---

3. *Details regarding visions, especially the imaginative vision*

27. — I will speak of those of Our Lord, following St. Teresa (*Interior Castle*, Sixth Mansion, chs. viii, ix; *Life*, ch. xxviii and following). We take it for granted that it is a question of visions that are really divine.

28. — 1° **Their object.** "... When Our Lord is pleased to caress the soul, He allows it in vision His Most Sacred Humanity, *under whatever form He chooses*; either as He was during His life on earth, or after His resurrection" (*Interior Castle*, Sixth Mansion, ch. ix, 2).

29. — 2° **At what times do they come?** Sometimes it is outside the time of the ecstasy, and they are then unexpected. Sometimes "a person is not thinking of seeing anything, nor has any such idea crossed the mind, when suddenly the vision is revealed in its entirety, causing within the powers and senses of the soul a fright and confusion which soon afterwards change into a blissful peace" (*Interior Castle*, Sixth Mansion, ch. ix, 7).

At other times the imaginative vision occurs during the ecstasy, or even produces it. "The former vision, which, as I said, represented God without any likeness of Him, is of a higher kind. . . . These two... visions come almost always together, and they do so come; for we behold the excellency and beauty and glory of the Most

Holy Humanity with the eyes of the soul. And in the other way I have spoken of — that of intellectual vision — we learn how He is God, is mighty, can do all things, commands all things, governs all things, and fills all things with His love" (*Life*, ch. xxviii, 14).

"… So exceedingly great is the power of this vision, when Our Lord shows the soul much of His grandeur and majesty, that it is impossible, in my opinion, for any soul to endure it, if Our Lord did not succor it in a most supernatural way, by throwing it into a trance or ecstasy whereby the vision of the divine presence is lost in the fruition thereof" (*Life*, ch. xxviii, 14).

30. — If the imaginative vision occurs when there is no ecstasy, does it always **produce** it? No. There is no necessity that the one should bring about the other. For St. John of the Cross speaks of these visions as "… that supernatural light, wherein he beholds what God wills, most easily and most distinctly, whether they be things of heaven or of earth; neither is their presence nor absence any impediment to the vision" (*Ascent of Mount Carmel*, Book II, ch. xxiv, p. 171). It should be so more especially when the apparition only lasts a moment (**33**). St. Teresa merely says, when speaking of imaginative visions of Our Lord, that the ecstasy "*almost* always" follows (see Extracts, **37**).

St. Thomas, on the other hand, seems to say that there is necessarily a certain alienation of one of the sensible faculties — that of sight. Otherwise, he says, "we should confuse the subject of the vision with other bodies" situated in the same direction (*Summa Theologiae*, II-II, q. 173, art. 3, c.). But to this we can reply that to obviate this drawback all that is necessary is to keep the eyes closed. As the holy Doctor must have foreseen such a simple answer, we must believe that he does not take the word *alienation* in its strict sense of a failure of the power of sight, but that he has stretched it so as to include any hindrance to its action proceeding from an external cause.

But even if the eyes are open, God has two very simple means of preventing this unfortunate confusion of two different impressions. The first consists in the brilliancy of the vision. It will then eclipse the rival sensation, just as the sun's splendor prevents our seeing the stars during the daytime, although our eyes still receive their rays. So, too, when the light of a lamp shines strongly in our eyes it prevents our distinguishing the objects in a dimly lighted room. We can imagine that it would be the same in the contest between two visual objects — one interior, the other exterior.

There is a second way also. When I fix my eyes upon some neighboring object, even when such an object is transparent, the things that are beyond it or on this side of it seem merely a confused mass that hardly distracts my attention. This is due to what is called the mechanism of adjustment of the eyes to different distances (by a convergence of the optical axes and a change in the curvature of the crystalline lens). During an interior vision the open eyes may, therefore, by the act of adjustment, interrupt their connection with any distant objects that would be a hindrance to them; and as this adjustment is habitual to them, it may readily be believed that they will perform it easily and suddenly. In this way God would not need to suspend any natural law.

31. — Inversely, when an imaginative vision produces alienation of the sensible faculties, does this state always contain the mystic union **over and above the vision**, and while the vision lasts? This is a question that no writer has ever set himself to solve, and it is one that is not cleared up by anything that we read in the saints' lives.

The question comes back to this: Are supernatural ecstasies always of the type described as having the mystic union as their foundation? We do not know.

32. — 3° **Reality of imaginative visions.** "Now and then it seemed to me that what I saw was an image; but *most frequently* it was not so. I thought it was Christ *Himself,* judging by the brightness in which He was pleased to show Himself. Sometimes the vision was so indistinct, that I thought it was an image, but still not like a picture, however well painted.... If what I saw was an image, it was a living image — not a dead man, but the *living* Christ: and He makes me see that He is *God and Man*... as He was when He had... risen from the dead.... No one can have any doubt that it is Our Lord Himself, especially after Communion: we know that He is then present, for faith says so" (*Life*, ch. xxviii, 11, 12).

33. — 4° Duration. According to St. Teresa, "the vision of Him passes so quickly that it may be compared to a flash of lightning" (*Interior Castle*, Sixth Mansion, ch. ix, 2, and the *First Letter* (*Relation* VII, 4) to Fr. Rodrigo Alvarez, *Life*, p. 445).

"When anyone can *contemplate* this sight of Our Lord *for a long time*, I do not believe it is a vision, but rather some overmastering idea" (*Interior Castle*, Sixth Mansion, ch. ix, 5).

"God puts it [this light] before us so instantaneously, that we could not open our eyes in time to see it, if it were necessary for us to open them at all. But whether our eyes be open or shut, it makes no difference whatever" (*Life*, ch. xxviii, 8).

St. John of the Cross speaks of imaginative visions in the same way: "When these visions occur, it is as if a door were opened into a most marvellous light, whereby the soul sees, as men do when the lightning suddenly *flashes* in a dark night. The lightning makes surrounding objects visible for an instant, and then leaves them in obscurity, though the forms of them remain in the fancy [i.e. the imagination]" (*Ascent of Mount Carmel*, Book II, ch. xxiv, p. 171).

We may ask ourselves, however, whether this impermanence is a general law. For the lives of the saints rarely exhibit this circumstance, and, on the contrary, they often seem to describe a persistence of these visions. And, further, in those cases where a picture of some historic fact, such as the Passion, passes before the eyes of the person in the ecstasy, it is certain that the scene takes some considerable length of time to unfold.

In the same way I have heard from several favored persons that their imaginative visions were prolonged, for some minutes, at least, especially when Our Lord spoke to them. One says that these apparitions (sometimes vague, sometimes very distinct) at times produced a fairly deep absorption, but this without, as a rule, hindering him from going and coming and carrying on his occupations (see **30**). He adds that this state is *not* accompanied by the mystic union (see **31**).

In the life of Sister Gojoz, of the Order of the Visitation, in the seventeenth century, it is said that she had a vision of Our Blessed Lord's Sacred Humanity that lasted for three years consecutively. He kept at her side. This vision was not exterior, however, for we are told that it was perceived by the "eye of the soul." It appears to have been imaginative and not intellectual, for it revealed "traits of the rarest beauty" and garments that did not bear the tint of any earthly colorings. "The most cloudless sun seemed obscure after the light that surrounded my Lord Jesus" (*Vie*, by Mère de Provane, Part II, ch. viii).

34. — "This vision [St. Teresa is speaking of intellectual visions]. . . unlike an imaginary one, does not pass away quickly, but lasts for several days, and even sometimes for a year... a most tender love for Him results from being constantly in His company.... Our Lord makes the soul conscious that He is close at hand" (*Interior Castle*, Sixth Mansion, ch. viii, 3, 6).

We have seen (**16**) that St. Teresa had intellectual visions of the Sacred Humanity before she had imaginative visions. I know a person whose case is the same. This may cause surprise, for the intellectual visions are of a higher order. But, on the other hand, they are less distinct. There has been progress, therefore, in the sense of distinctness. What confirms this idea is that the same process of gradual development was followed in the case of St. Teresa's imaginative visions. First she saw only Our Lord's Hands, then His Face, and finally the whole Body (*Life*, ch. xxviii).

34 bis. — 5° These visions possess **great beauty** and perfection. "So beautiful are glorified bodies, that the glory which surrounds them renders those who see that which is so supernatural and beautiful beside themselves.... If I were to spend many years in devising how to picture to myself anything so beautiful, I should never be able, nor even know how, to do it; for it is beyond the reach of any possible imagination here below: the whiteness and brilliancy alone are inconceivable" (*Life*, ch. xxviii, 3, 7).

The vividness of her visions contrasts with the difficulty that she had in her ordinary state, in picturing Our Lord to herself.

35. — Although certain details are shown with clarity, the imaginative visions are sometimes **incomplete** in certain respects, and we cannot make them more perfect. "As to the vision of which I am speaking, there are no means of bringing it about; only we must behold it when Our Lord is pleased to present it before us, *as He wills* and what He wills; and there is no possibility of taking anything away from it, or of adding anything to it; nor is there any way of effecting it, whatever we may do, nor of seeing it when we like, nor of abstaining from seeing; if we try to gaze upon it — part of the vision in particular — the vision of Christ is lost at once.... I was extremely desirous to behold the color of His eyes, or the form of them, so that I might be able to describe them, yet I never attained to the sight of them, and I could do nothing for that end; on the contrary, I lost the vision altogether" (*Life*, ch. xxix, 1, 2).

In the imaginative vision "it is no more possible to *continue looking at it* [the vision of Our Lord's Humanity], than to gaze for a long time on the sun" (*Interior Castle*, Sixth Mansion, ch. ix, 2).

So, too, intellectual visions may be very clear or partially obscure. St. Teresa speaks of the first only. Our Lord, she says, "renders Himself present to the soul by a certain knowledge of Himself which is more clear than the sun" (*Life*, ch. xxvii, 5). Alvarez de Paz describes the obscure kind of vision (see Extracts, 49).

36. — 6° **Certainty.** "The soul *for some time afterwards* possesses such certainty that this grace comes from God, that, whatever people may say to the contrary, it cannot fear a delusion. Later on, when her confessor suggests doubts to her, God may allow such a person to waver in her belief for a time, and to feel misgivings, lest, in punishment for her sins, she may possibly have been left to go astray. However, she does not give way to these apprehensions, but (as I said in speaking of other matters) they only affect her in the same way as the temptations of the Devil against faith, which may disturb the mind, but do not shake the firmness of belief. In fact, the more the evil one assails her with fears, the more certain does she feel that he could never have produced the great benefits she is conscious of having received, because *he exercises no such power over the interior of the soul.* He may present a false apparition, but it does not possess the *truth, operations,* and *efficacy* of the one she has seen" (*Interior Castle,* Sixth Mansion, ch. ix, 8).

37. — 7° **What are the sentiments produced by these visions?** The Divine Master causes "within the powers and senses of the soul a fright and conclusion which soon afterwards change into a blissful peace. Thus, after St. Paul was thrown prostrate on the ground, a great tempest and noise followed from Heaven; so, in the interior world of the soul, there is a violent tumult, followed instantly, as I have said, by perfect calm" (*ibid.,* 7).

"The soul to whom God grants this vision almost always falls into an ecstasy, nature being too weak to bear so *dread* a sight. I say 'dread,' although this apparition is more *lovely* and *delightful* than anything that could be imagined, even though one lived a thousand years, and spent all that time in trying to picture it, for it far surpasses the limits of our imagination and understanding; yet the presence of such surpassing majesty inspires the soul with *great fear*" (*ibid.,* 3).

St. John of the Cross says: "The effects which these (imaginative) visions in the soul produce are quiet, illumination, *joy* like that of glory, *sweetness,* purity and love, humility and the inclination or *elevation of the mind to God,* sometimes more, sometimes less, sometimes more of one, sometimes more of another, according to the disposition of the soul and the will of God... [T]hose of Satan result in *dryness of spirit,* in a tendency to self-esteem... and in no degree whatever do they produce the *gentleness* of humility and love of God.... [They are] remembered... with great *aridity of spirit,* and without the fruit of humility and love which issue out of the good visions whenever they are recalled" (*Ascent of Mount Carmel*, Book II, ch. xxiv, pp. 171-172).

38. — 8° *Observance of propriety in the visions.* "There never was anything in any of these spiritual visitations that was not wholly pure and clean, nor does she think it can be otherwise if the spirit be good and the visitations supernatural" (*Relation* VII, 23; *Life*, p. 453).

"The raiment worn by the Person seen, looks like fine linen" (*Interior Castle*, Sixth Mansion, ch. ix, 3).

"These satanic visions are very different things… the joy which Satan ministers must be, I think, very different — it shows *no traces of pure and holy love*" (*Life*, ch. xxviii, 15). See Chapter Three, **34**.

39. — 9° **A wide range of knowledge.** "Certain sublime truths have been so impressed upon the mind that it needs no other Master" (*Interior Castle*, Sixth Mansion, ch. ix, 7). The saint explains elsewhere (*Life*, ch. xxvi, 6) how Our Lord became a "living book" to her by these visions.

In the visions many kinds of knowledge may be simultaneously received. St. Alphonsus Rodriguez relates that, being transported to Heaven in an ecstasy, "he saw and knew *all* the Blessed together, and each one of them separately, as if he had passed his *whole life* with them" (*Vie*, from his Memoirs, Appendix No. 275).

And the same thing happened with regard to the angels (No. 6; see also 52, 148). It is related of St. Bridget that she often, in one single instant of time, saw all the inhabitants of Heaven, Earth, and Hell, and perceived what each was saying to the other (*Revelations, Prologue*, by Alphonsus de Vadatera, ch. iv).

With regard to the variety of the knowledge acquired by means of visions, we may cite St. Lidwine. Nearly every night for twenty-eight years she had an ecstasy, lasting an hour, during which time she was conveyed to Heaven, to Purgatory, to Hell, or to a great variety of places, such as the Holy Land, Rome, etc., where she venerated the relics of the saints; and also to a great many churches and monasteries, the situations of which she knew and the names of the inhabitants (Bolland., April 14, ch. v).

The counterfeits of the imagination have no power to increase our knowledge in this way.

40. — 10° Effects upon the conduct. "... For as there were most holy persons in the place... whom God did not lead by this way, they [Fr. Balthasar Alvarez and those whom he told her to consult] were at once filled with fear; they thought it all came through my sins. And so my state was talked about and came to the knowledge of many.... I said to them once... [that] all who knew me saw clearly that *my soul was changed* — and so my confessor said; for the *difference* was *very great* in every way — not a pretence, but such as all might most clearly observe. As I was formerly so wicked, I said, I could not believe that Satan, if he wished to deceive me and take me down to hell, would have recourse to means so adverse to his purpose as this of *rooting out my faults,* implanting *virtues and spiritual strength,* for I saw clearly that I had become *at once* another person through the instrumentality of these visions" (*Life*, ch. xxviii, 18, 19).

"And it is from this it comes to pass that he in whom God works these graces [visions of Our Lord] despises himself, and becomes *more humble* than he ever was before, for he sees that this is a gift of God, and that he can neither add to it nor take from it. The love and the desire become greater of serving Our Lord..." (*Relation* VII, 26, made for Fr. Rodrigo Alvarez, *Life*, pp. 454-455).

41. — 11° Persistent memory. "... This most glorious picture makes an impression on the imagination, that I believe can never be effaced until the soul at last sees Christ, to enjoy Him for ever." While, on the other hand, illusory visions "pass from the memory more quickly than do dreams" (*Interior Castle*, Sixth Mansion, ch. ix, 2, 6).

4. Various Questions

42. — Let us speak first of the nature of exterior or corporeal visions (whether of divine or diabolic origin). They may be produced in **four different ways:**

First manner, which is objective. The body is really that of the person appearing; it is *its substance* that acts upon our eyes.

This case cannot occur with angels and disembodied spirits, as they have no bodies. But we can conceive of this mode as possible for Our Lord and the Blessed Virgin, whose bodies and souls are in Heaven, and also for a living man who might appear to us.

In such a circumstance, the body, although real, may not retain its natural appearance. It was thus that Our Lord showed Himself to St. Mary Magdalen, after His Resurrection, in the likeness of a gardener, and to the disciples at Emmaus as a traveller. And yet it was His real Body that was perceived. Only His garments may have lacked actuality. Even in His appearances to the apostles, Christ did not allow all the splendor and beauty of His glorified Body to appear.

Second manner, which is also objective. A body exists materially, but it is a borrowed body, and it is then admittedly formed by the ministry of angels. God thus makes use of secondary causes for works which they are capable of executing.

Third manner, which may be called semi-objective. There is no longer any true body, but there is still something material outside the person who sees it, namely, luminous rays, similar to those that a body would have been capable of emitting. The angels produce these undulations as they would produce sound waves, and they cause them to travel from the place that the object is supposed to occupy. At times it would even be sufficient for them to utilize, by diverting them, the diffused rays of the surrounding light. And as the eye of the person who sees the vision will then receive the light in a natural way, as occurred in the above-mentioned cases, the pupil will be lit up as it would be before any brilliant object, and will reflect the picture before it. The bystanders might be able to see the reflection, which has the appearance of a finely wrought cameo. I know two ecstatics in whose cases this phenomena has often been verified.

Fourth manner, which is purely subjective. The angels imprint the image of the object directly upon the retina.

St. Thomas (*Summa Theologiae*, III, q. 76, art. 8, c.) describes these different manners with the exception of the third. He could not imagine this one on account of the theories current in his day on the subject of light. It was not then understood to be a vibration, something that propagates itself, and of which the movement may be brought about artificially, without the qualities of a real body.

43. — St. Thomas admits that the last manner is rather **less probable** when all who are present see the apparition. The other means seem to give the simplest explanation of the phenomenon.

When, however, the seer of the vision is the only one to perceive the apparition, St. Thomas is inclined to think that the vision is purely subjective. The following explanation may be given: if the luminous rays existed (and this would be the case in the three first modes), God would have to prevent their reaching the other persons who are present. This would seem to be multiplying miracles without necessity.

But for many visions we are reduced to mere conjectures. At Lourdes, for instance, Bernadette was the only one to see and hear the Blessed Virgin. It cannot be decided with any certainty which of the four above-mentioned modes was employed.

44. — **Actual personal presence in corporeal apparitions.** Theologians have discussed the question as to whether, since His Ascension, or at least since His appearance to St. Paul on the way to Damascus, Christ has shown Himself in the first manner — that is to say, with the substance of His Body. It would take too long to go into all the conflicting opinions and the reasons of congruity that have been brought forward to support them. M. Ribet has carried out this task (Vol. II, ch. vi). Like Suarez (*De incarn.*, disp.

51, a. 4, sect. iv), he is inclined to admit that this kind of .... may have occurred. He adds: "St. Teresa seems to favor the contrary opinion (*Additions* to her *Life*); but she relies less on the revelations that she had received than on the conclusions that she drew from them." And these conclusions may have been influenced by the theological opinions of her directors.

45. — There is a **point** the decision of which is much **more important.** Whether it is or is not the actual Flesh of the Sacred Humanity that we see, is for us a question of but secondary importance. But have we *really* to do with His *Person*, or only with one of His envoys? This is what is meant when we inquire whether the apparition is personal. It is this, above all, that we wish to know.

There is no difficulty if Our Lord shows Himself in close proximity to the Sacred Host. But in other cases there are two opinions. According to the first, there is a purely moral presence only, that of the King who is represented by his ambassador. Briefly, the apparition would merely be produced upon an order given to an angel by Our Lord, the Blessed Virgin, or a saint, and there would be no further link than this between them and the seer of the vision.

It is further added that the reverence and love shown towards the image are legitimate. For these sentiments merely pass through the image, so to speak, and go to the person whom it represents.

The contrary opinion holds that something more than this is present, and that it can be called a real presence, although it is not possible to state its nature exactly. We should *really enter into relation* with the saint who appeared: just as when we come in contact with the sun's rays we really enter into relation with the sun; but it is far otherwise when we look at a picture representing it.

This doctrine of a *personal action* is the only one that seems probable to me. It is held by all the saints who have seen corporeal apparitions. They have never imagined that they had before them, or that they held in their arms, a mere statue, only differing from others by the perfection of color or movement. This is evident from their accounts of what had passed and from their actions. For example: St. Anthony of Padua covered the Infant Jesus with his kisses. It was certainly a question here of a corporeal apparition, for he touched the Holy Child, and the scene was witnessed by the owner of the house where the saint lodged. St. Peter, at the gate of Rome, threw himself at the feet of the apparition (which argues that it was corporeal), saying the well-known words: "*Quo vadis, Domine?*" "Lord, where are You going?" This phrase would have had no meaning if he had thought that he was speaking to a mere image.

Finally, it has often happened that the saints have been confirmed in this conviction by the language uttered by the apparition. It said: "I am such or such a saint," not "I represent such or such a saint." None but Jesus Christ could reply to St. Peter: "I am going to be crucified in Rome."

St. Thomas admits the same opinion by implication. For he asks (*loc. cit.*) if God does not deceive the seer of the vision when He gives a borrowed body to a saint, since the appearance is so perfect that it cannot be distinguished from the reality. But he replies to this difficulty in the negative only when it is a question of Christ and of an apparition in close proximity to the Sacred Host. For, according to him, the borrowed form then exhibits a reality, an actual presence. Such a reply implies that if there were not always a certain presence of Christ or of the saint, the seer of the vision would be misled by God.

46. — In the lives of several saints we see that they received graces which are, as it were, lesser examples of revelations properly so called, the **infused knowledge**, that is to say, of certain religious questions, the meaning of passages in the Bible, for instance. St. Teresa says that she received them at times (*Life*, ch. xv, 12).

What is the exact nature of this gift? I am inclined to think that, in general, it is not a question of really scientific knowledge, or historical information fitted to dispel the uncertainties of exegesis, or of new dogmatic views. For we do not find that the greater number of these communications have been transmitted to scholars, in the strict sense of the word. God's aim is a more practical one. He gives thoughts conducive to piety, analogies that elevate the soul; and in order to do this, in the case of the Holy Scriptures, all that is necessary, is to reveal some appropriate meaning.

47. — Many saints, such as St. Catherine of Siena, the Ven. Ursula Benincasa, St. Catherine of Ricci (*Vie*, by Fr. Bayonne, Vol. I, ch. viii), have received a grace that is called **change of heart**. We do not know its nature. Something takes place in the material heart. Is it a real modification or a simple impression? The saints have not explained this point. It is always the symbol of a new life for the soul, or even, perhaps, for the body.

And, equally, other saints have spoken of entering **into the Heart of Jesus**, or into the Wound in His Sacred Side. Are these metaphorical expressions to indicate the contemplation of His love, of His sufferings, or even of His Divinity? Or is it a mysterious grace, of a kind apart? We have no material by which to decide this question either.

EXTRACTS
Description and Object of Intellectual Visions

---

48. — St. Teresa:
1° Speaking of herself: "She sees nothing either outwardly or inwardly… but without seeing anything, she understands *what* it is, and *where* it is, *more clearly than if she saw it*, only nothing in particular presents itself to her. She is like a person who *feels* that another is close beside her; but because she is *in the dark* she sees him not… without a word, inward or outward, the soul *clearly perceives* who it is, where he is and occasionally what he means. Why or how she perceives it, she knows not; but so it is" (*Relation* VII, 26, to Fr. Rodrigo Alvarez, *Life*, p. 454). See also the simile of the

diamond in the closed casket (*Interior Castle*, Sixth Mansion, ch. ix, 1). In the imaginative vision the casket is open.

2° Still speaking of herself: "Her confessor… asked her how, if she saw nothing, she knew that Our Lord was near her, and bade her describe His appearance. She said she was unable to, for she could not see His face, nor could she tell more than she had already said, but that she was sure she was right, and that it was He who spoke to her. . . . You will ask: 'If we see no one, how can we know whether it is Christ, or His most glorious Mother, or a saint?' One cannot answer this question, or *know* how one distinguishes them, but the fact remains *undoubted*" (*Interior Castle*, Sixth Mansion, ch. viii, 3, 8).

3° "Jesus Christ seemed to be by my side continually, and as the vision was not imaginary, *I saw no form*" (*Life*, ch. xxvii, 3).

4° "She was conscious of His being at her right hand, although not in the way we know an ordinary person to be beside us, but in a more sublime manner which I cannot describe. This Presence is, however, quite as evident and certain, and indeed far more so, than the ordinary presence of other people. About this we may be deceived, but not in that" (*Interior Castle*, Sixth Mansion, ch. viii, 4).

5° "It is very rarely that I saw Satan assume a bodily form; I know of his presence through the vision I have spoken of before, the vision wherein *no form* is seen" (*Life*, ch. xxxi, 10).

6° "Multitudes of angels seemed to me to be above the canopies of the stalls… but I saw no bodily forms, for the vision was intellectual" (*Relation* III, 16; *Life*, p. 429).

7° When one of the cherubim "his face burning," pierced the saint's heart with "a long spear of gold, and at the iron's point there seemed to be a little fire," she saw him on her "left side, in bodily form." The vision was an imaginative one. For intellectually we cannot see a body that does not really exist, and we have said (**16**, 5°) that the saint never saw visions with her bodily eyes. Further, she particularly says that this was so, for she adds, when speaking of the borrowed form that was thus represented to her: "This [the bodily form] I am not accustomed to see, unless very rarely. Though

I have visions of angels frequently, yet I see them *only as an intellectual vision*, such as I have spoken of before" (*Life*, ch. xxix, 16, 17).

49. — Alvarez de Paz:

He says that with intellectual visions some are very distinct, and others, on the contrary, are confused. If we see Jesus Christ or the Blessed Virgin in the second manner, "we see nothing formed, with regard either to the face or the body, and yet we know more certainly than by the evidence of the eyes that the person in question is either at your right hand or in your heart.... It is as though you were suddenly, *in the darkness*, to feel that someone is beside you, and to know that goodwill and not enmity is felt towards you; but you are quite ignorant as to whether it is a man or a woman, whether young or old, good-looking or no, and whether standing or sitting."[9] The writer adds: "Perhaps you would like to know whether we see the person who appears thus intellectually, as he really is? I reply that with regard to the angels, they show themselves present really and by their substance." As for Our Lord's Body, in order to be seen close to us intellectually, there is no need for Him to leave Heaven, for "a sound philosophy teaches us that God can, in the absence of an object, represent it to us just as it would appear if it were present" (*De inquisitione pacis*, Book V, Part III, ch. xii).

Notes

¹ In French [as in English] it is the custom to say *imaginary* locutions and visions, following the Latin. If I make this change it is because in our language the word *imaginary* nearly always means a flight of the imagination; it applies to things that are entirely nonexistent, while *imaginative* means an act of the imagination, but one that is not inordinate. The word *imaginary* is often wrongly understood by the uninstructed in these matters, because they take it in the everyday sense.

² Taken alone this last word is ambiguous. It might only mean to signify that the *object* of the vision is corporeal. But it is also intended to point to the exterior *mode* of vision, to the exclusion of the two following modes.

[3] At this period Fr. Balthazar Alvarez was her confessor. He continued to act in this capacity for seven years, but he was only raised to mystic contemplation later, in 1567, a year after his departure from Avila, when he was thirty-four years of age and had just been professed (*Life* by the Ven. L. du Pont, ch. xiii). The result was that while at Avila he did not completely understand the saint's state, and he became doubtful when he found that everyone was condemning her visions. She says: "This great humility of his brought me into serious trouble, for though he was a man much given to prayer, and learned, he never trusted his own judgment, because *Our Lord was not leading him by this way*" (*Life*, ch. xxviii, 20). Later on, ten years after he had received the grace of contemplation (1577), he was obliged to defend his method of prayer against some violent attacks made against it (see ch. xiv, **32** [of *The Graces of Interior Prayer*]).

    St. Teresa gives a list of her principal directors in her *First Letter* to Fr. Rodrigo Alvarez (1576) (*Relation*, VII, *Life*, p. 446).

[4] The Ven. Mary of the Incarnation, an Ursuline nun, at the age of fifty-two was favored for some considerable time with an intellectual vision of the Blessed Virgin. She was thus assisted during the reconstruction of her Convent at Quebec (*Vie*, by an Ursuline of Nantes, ch. xv).

[5] Schizophrenic patients who think they hear voices do not generally feel this joy. The words are disagreeable, aggressive, and usually take the form of an obsession. Further, these persons have not the feeling of conviction, for by their very nature they are doubters.

[6] The same fact is related with regard to St. Bridget by one of her secretaries (*Prologue*, by Alphonsus de Vadatera, ch. iv). He affirms that she received the whole of the fifth book of her revelations instantaneously, with the Rule of her Order, which occupies forty folio columns (Roman ed., 1628). St. Hildegard says that everything that she learned with regard to human affairs was always given "as though instantaneously" (Migne ed., col. 18, A).

[7] He gives them the name of *Formal Words*, which in no way suggests the quality that he attributes to them by definition, that of effecting little without the active participation of the mind.

[8] With regard to the words that are heard, as it were, within our own breast, the writer supposes that there is a sound perceived by the imaginative faculty. We must not confuse this case with that which is observed in certain mental wards. There is no sound, but only the movement of an interior organ, which has the same result. The sick person experiences involuntary movements of the tongue, or the larynx, the throat or the lungs, identical with those that would take place if he pronounced the words aloud. These motor perceptions suggest to him (with the help, perhaps, of arbitrary interpretations) corresponding ideas, as would be the case with words either heard or real. Consequently the sick man wrongly imagines himself to be entering into conversation with a mysterious being, whether a friend or an enemy. This is what is called *kinesthetic language*, in contradistinction to *audible* and *visual*.

[9] Here is an example of the obscure intellectual vision — one, that is to say, giving a very incomplete manifestation of the qualities of the object seen. A person wrote to me as follows: "I had a sister who lived at a great distance from me and who died very young, after a short illness. The day of her death, of which I was wholly

unaware, I suddenly began to tremble. I experienced in a quite indefinable manner the impression that someone, some soul, was gazing at my soul. I had not the impression that the soul was suffering, but on the contrary it appeared to me to be wholly filled with joy and all inflamed with love. Not knowing that manifestations of this nature were possible, I tried to reject this impression. But it persisted all afternoon, although less distinctly. I felt that this someone remained in my company, on my left hand and a little in front of me. For the next two or three days the impression was still weaker. And then it suddenly seemed to me that this invisible being was leaving me in order to ascend to Heaven, there to obtain the graces that I was beginning to receive. Who was it? I was only able to guess at the answer later, when learning the coincidence of the death and of my impression."

CHAPTER TWO

ILLUSIONS TO BE AVOIDED

1. — We distinguish **two kinds** of revelations. The one kind, called *universal,* is contained in the Bible or in the deposit of the apostolic tradition, and is transmitted by the organ of the Church. This came to an end with the preaching of the apostles, and is a matter of faith for everyone. The other is called *special* or *private.* This has always taken place among Christians. I need only concern myself with this latter kind.

2. — With regard to the special revelations that have been made to the saints, **belief** in them is **not required** by the Church even when she approves them. By this approbation she only intends to declare that nothing is to be found in them contrary to faith or morals, and that they can be accepted without danger and even with advantage. "It matters little," says Melchior Cano, "whether or no one believes in St. Bridget's revelations or those of other saints, these things have nothing to do with faith" (*De locis theologicis,* Book XII, ch. iii).

Benedict XIV is quite clear with regard to this question. "What is to be said of those private revelations which the Apostolic See has *approved* of, those of the Blessed Hildegard [which were approved in part by Eugene III], of St. Bridget [by Boniface IX], and of St. Catherine of Siena [by Gregory XI]? We have already said that those revelations, although approved of, ought not to, and cannot, receive from us any assent of Catholic, but only of *human faith*, according to the rules of prudence, according to which the aforesaid revelations are *probable*, and *piously to be believed* [*probabiles et piè credibles*]" (*De canon.*, Book III, ch. liii, No. 15; Book II, ch. xxxii, No. 11. Eng. trans.: *Benedict XIV on Heroic Virtue*, Vol. III, ch. xiv).

Cardinal Pitra says the same: "Everyone knows that we are fully at liberty to believe or not to believe in private revelations, even those most worthy of credence. Even when the Church *approves* them, they are merely received as *probable*, and not as indubitable. They are not to be used as *deciding* questions of history, natural philosophy, philosophy, or theology which are matters of controversy between the Doctors. It is quite permissible to differ from these revelations, even when approved, if we are relying upon solid reasons, and especially if the contrary doctrine is proved by unimpeachable documents and definite experience" (Book on St. Hildegard, p. xvi).

The Bollandists lay down the same principles (May 25, p. 243, No. 246, and *Parergon*, p. 246, No. 1).

Granted that the Church assumes no further responsibility, a question then arises: "What is the last word regarding the actual authority of private revelations? They have the value of the testimony of the person who witnesses to having received them, neither more nor less. Now, this person is never infallible: it is evident, then, that the points vouched for are never absolutely certain — except in the sole case where a miracle is worked directly in favor of the attestation. In a word, private revelations have only a purely human or probable authority" (Fr. Toulemont on *Private revelations* in the Review, *Les Études*, 1866, p. 61).

3. — After perusing these passages, the reader will be less astonished when we say that even the revelations of the saints may contain errors occasionally.

I will now endeavor to classify the different kinds of illusions that are to be feared. But first I must warn the reader against two **exaggerated conclusions** that he might be inclined to draw from the pages about to follow:

1° Seeing that the causes of illusion are numerous and difficult to avoid completely, he will perhaps conclude that all revelations should be rejected without examination. No. Wisdom lies in
the middle course: we should neither believe nor reject unless we
have sufficient proofs: lacking such, we must not pronounce any
opinion.

2° As examples of these illusions I will choose, by preference,
those of the saints or other pious persons.[1] It must not be concluded
that the saints are always or even often mistaken. The instances of
errors are not frequent; and where they occur they are not of any
great importance.

And further, if one of their revelations be false, it does not
follow that it should be the same with their ecstasies, for ecstasy is
much less subject to illusion.

In making this selection, I have not acted in any captious spirit
and with the object of diminishing the respect that we owe to the
saints, but for a grave reason of utility.[2] It is the best way of persuading certain pious persons to mistrust their own revelations, and
of persuading their directors to do the same. If I were to quote cases
of none but quite ordinary souls, people would say: "Yes, certainly
illusions are to be feared; but for ignorant people and beginners.
As for the instructed and clear-sighted, they escape, especially when
they are pious and of more than ordinary virtue (we always rank
ourselves amongst the select few). If this were otherwise, God, who
is so good, would be betraying the trust that we put in Him." But
if this argument were applicable in our own case, it would be much
more necessarily so still where the saints are in question. They were
far more enlightened than ourselves and were the object of a much
closer protection on God's part. And yet they have sometimes been
mistaken. The facts are before us.

But by this method there is no possible point of escape. All
must frankly apply to themselves the rules of prudence to be given
further on. We can no longer listen to the self-love that whispers:
"These rules are excellent, but they are not meant for you. You are
not like other men."

Practically, in the case of those who have not attained to high sanctity, we can admit that at least three-quarters of their revelations are illusions.

3 *bis.* — I am led to believe that illusion is easier in the case of interior locutions (intellectual or imaginative) than with imaginative visions. They are much more nearly allied to the ordinary operations of the human mind in which ideas and phrases arise perpetually. If these are clear and sudden, an inexperienced person will conclude that he cannot have produced them himself. The illusion is due principally to an interpretation based on insufficient facts. There has been no fundamentally new act. On the contrary, the interior visual illusions are very superior, both with regard to accuracy and intensity, to the current representations of the imagination. It is then more difficult, so it seems, to mistake one for the other.

These considerations also explain why certain persons, like St. Teresa (Chapter One, **16**), begin to hear divine locutions in the waking state, before being favored with any frequency, at least, with imaginative visions. It is that the first-named, as we have just said, are more closely allied to our own nature. God thus avoids too sudden transitions.

3 *ter.* — It is clear that revelations and visions are without danger and **very useful** if they are divine, for grace operates only for our welfare; and when it is likewise of such an extraordinary order it cannot be destined for a merely ordinary good. Holy Scripture is filled with facts of this nature which have rendered great spiritual service. St. Teresa often explains that this has been so in her case. I give no example, the thesis being so evident.

The revelations that are due to Satan, on the other hand, always tend to produce evil or to hinder good. And, further, those produced by our own imagination are usually useless or dangerous.

It is very important, therefore, in such a matter to learn to distinguish the true and the certain from the false or the doubtful. This will be the object of this chapter and the two succeeding ones.

1. Five causes of error that may have had an influence upon true revelations, or revelations regarded as such, at certain periods and in certain countries.[3]

4. — These **five causes** of error are: 1° faulty interpretations of revelations or visions; 2° ignorance of the fact that historic events are often given with approximate truth only; 3° the mingling of human activity with supernatural action during the revelation; 4° the subsequent, but involuntary, modifications made by the person who receives the revelation; and, finally, 5° embellishments by secretaries or compilers of the Life.

5. — *First cause of error.* A divine **revelation** may at times be **interpreted wrongly** by the person who receives it.

6. — This may be due primarily to the **obscurity** of the revelation. God at times gives only a **partial comprehension** of its import. His communication has a deep meaning that is not understood; it is taken in the everyday sense.

St. John of the Cross says on this subject: "... many prophecies and Divine locutions disappointed, in their fulfillment, the expectations of many of the ancient people, because they understood them *too much according to the letter* in their own way.... This is the way in which many souls deceive themselves in the matter of revelations and Divine locutions. They understand them *in the letter according to their apparent meaning.* For, as I have said, the chief purpose of God in sending visions is to express and communicate the Spirit which is hidden within them, and which is very hard to be understood. This is much more abundant than the letter, more extraordinary, and surpasses the limits thereof" (*Ascent of Mount Carmel,* Book II, ch. xix, pp. 133-136).

Like St. John of the Cross, Scaramelli cites various examples drawn from ancient history (Tr. 4, ch. xviii). To give a more recent instance, let us take the words heard by **St. Joan of Arc** in prison. She says in her examination: "I inquired of my voices whether I should be burned; and they answered me that I should trust in Our Lord, and that *He would aid me....* St. Catherine told me that I should *receive succor.*" Joan states that she interprets this utterance as indicating her deliverance. She adds: "As a rule, the voices tell me that I shall be *delivered by a great victory.* And afterwards they say: 'Fear not because of your *martyrdom.* It will bring you at last to Paradise.'" These predictions were quite accurate. But Joan did not see their real significance. She thought, as she herself explains, that the word *martyrdom* meant "the great pains and adversity that she suffered in prison"; and the "deliverance by a great victory" caused her to think of something quite different to her death.[4]

7. — In one of **St. Mechtildis'** revelations, we have an example of an interpretation that seems to be inaccurate. Her pupil, St. Gertrude, had asked her to pray that she might obtain "the virtues of docility and patience that she thought herself to need." St. Mechtildis related Our Lord's utterances to her on the subject, saying that Gertrude already possessed these virtues, and adding words of encouragement that concluded thus: "The patience (*patientia*) that pleases Me in her, derives its name from *pax* and *scientia* (peace and knowledge). She must so apply herself to patience as never to lose *peace* of heart in adversity, and have the *knowledge* that consists in knowing why she suffers: it is through love and as a mark of inviolable fidelity" (*Le Héraut de l'amour divin*, Book I, ch. xvi). The saint would have been right if she had understood these words as signifying that St. Gertrude's patience *had its source* in peace and knowledge, or again, that the word *patience* ought to remind her of two others; but the ambiguous words, "Patience *derives* its name..." seem rather to suggest that the saint understood it to be a question of the actual etymology, a historic connection between these different words. If she accepted them in this sense, as Amort believes her to have done (Part II, ch. viii, 3), she was mistaken. For philologists know that the root of *patientia* has no relation to the word *pax.* Our Lord did not wish to give her a lesson in philology, but to remind her of a useful counsel.

So, too, **St. Gertrude** relates that on Easter Sunday Our Lord said to her, when speaking of the word *Alleluia*: "Observe that all the vowels, except the *o*, which signifies grief, are found in this word; and that, instead of this *o*, the *a* is repeated twice." And then follows a description of the joys of the risen Christ that the saint could associate with each vowel (Book IV, ch. xxvii). The revelation may be a true one, if it is a question of a conventional signification given to the letter *o*. But by itself, as Amort remarks, this vowel serves as well to express pleasure as grief (Part II, ch. viii, 10); and the others express grief equally with pleasure. However, it may have been otherwise in the language that the saint herself spoke. But even so, we must not turn what is simply a pious expedient for fixing the attention, into a philological decision.

8. — We have seen that there is sometimes only a partial understanding of a divine revelation; but cases may be quoted where it is even less than this. God does not make the meaning of the vision appear at all at first. Thus Pharaoh and his two servants had to have recourse to Joseph to interpret their prophetic dreams [Genesis 40-41]. Nebuchadnezzar could not even recall the dream of the statue with the feet of clay. Daniel was obliged to repeat all the details to him; he did this, pointing out that such a supernatural knowledge was the sign of the truth of his interpretation. Daniel was likewise the only one to understand the king's other dream: that of the tree which was cut down and of which the stump alone was left, and the vision of Belshazzar's feast [Daniel 4-5].

These visions were sent by God to men who were sinners, and those of the saints have sometimes been as unintelligible to them for a time. When **St. Peter** had the vision of the linen sheet containing all manner of beasts, a voice said to him three times: "Get up, Peter; kill and eat." He thought the words referred to his food, all the more because the ecstasy came upon him when he was hungry and a meal was being prepared for him (Acts 10:10). He did not see the true meaning, which was symbolic; namely, the command to baptize the Gentiles without first laying upon them the ordinances enjoined by the Mosaic Law. He strove vainly to understand (*dum intra se haesitaret*, 10:17). The significance only came to him two days later, when called to Caesarea to the Centurion Cornelius, who wished to become a Christian (10:28).

9. — Or, again, false interpretations may arise, not from the obscurity of the revelation, but because, unknown to the person receiving it, it contains **conditions that are understood** but not expressed. It is wrong to take it unconditionally.

It was thus that Jonah, when preaching the destruction of Nineveh after forty days, was persuaded that it would be destroyed even if the inhabitants repented. God had decided otherwise, without acquainting him of the fact. On seeing that repentant Nineveh stood and was spared, he "was exceedingly troubled and was angry," and he prayed that he might die (Jonah 4:1).

Perhaps a false prophecy made by **St. Norbert**, founder of the Premonstratensians, may be explained in the same way. Here is St. Bernard's account of the circumstance (Migne ed., *Letter 56*; written about 1128): "I asked him what he knew about Antichrist. He declared that he knew by revelation and in a *very certain* way that he would come in this generation. As I did not share this belief, I asked him his reasons. His reply did not satisfy me. He tried at least to persuade me that he would not die without having seen a general persecution in the Church."

St. Vincent Ferrer offers us a yet more striking instance of conditions that must be understood, although they are not expressed in the prophecy. He spent the last twenty-one years of his life (1398-1419) announcing that the Last Judgment was *at hand*, in the everyday sense of the word. He had learned this by a very clear and unconditional vision,[5] the truth of which he proved by his numberless miracles. These had amounted, by his own showing, to more than three thousand when he came to preach at Salamanca (1412); it was here that he worked the most famous of all these prodigies in support of his preaching, bringing to life for the space of fifteen minutes a woman who was being carried to the cemetery, and who confirmed his predictions. And yet this prophecy has not been fulfilled. This fact is accounted for by saying that it was conditional. The time of the great Western Schism truly merited the end of the world as a chastisement. But this misfortune was averted by the wholesale conversions wrought throughout Europe among Catholics, heretics, Jews, and Moslems by the saint's threats and miracles.[6]

10. — We may believe that all **prophecies** of punishments to come are conditional; and it is the same with those **promising special favors.** As an example, we may give the promise concerning the Scapular. The Blessed Virgin appeared to St. Simon Stock, the sixth General of the Carmelites in 1251, at Cambridge, and said: "Whosoever shall die clothed in this Habit shall not suffer the eternal fires." Theologians hold that this phrase, though at first sight unconditional, is not to be interpreted too rigidly. It is true that very great graces are attached to the wearing of the Scapular, and that we thereby create a kind of right to the special protection of the Queen of Heaven. But if anyone were to reject the aids of religion on his deathbed, it is clear that he would not merit this protection and that he would be lost. It would be the same if a man relied upon this promise in order to plunge more completely into vice (see Fr. Terrien, *Marie, mère des hommes*, Book X, ch. i). Also, speaking of this revelation, Benedict XIV says: "She does not say that those who have worn the Scapular will be preserved from eternal fire *by this means alone*, without having done anything else. Good works and perseverance in well-doing are necessary to eternal salvation" (*De festis*, Part II, No. 96). He points out, with St. Robert Bellarmine, that Holy Scripture sometimes promises salvation in connection with practices that *cannot suffice by themselves*, such as faith, hope, almsgiving, Holy Communion.

So, too, many divine promises made to the religious Orders or to Confraternities suppose a cooperation, but this cooperation will be brought about by the great graces bestowed.

11. — *Second cause of error.* When visions represent **historic scenes**, those of the Life or Death of Our Lord, for instance, they often have an **approximate** and probable likeness only, although

no intimation of this circumstance is given. It is a mistake to attribute an absolute accuracy to them.

This is a very natural mistake. For, at first sight, it seems that, as the visions are divine, all their details should be the faithful reproduction of the event, as to scenery, dress, the words and gestures, etc. Many saints have, in fact, believed that the event depicted took place exactly as they saw it.

But God does not deceive us when He modifies certain details; If He tied Himself down to absolute accuracy in these matters, we should soon be seeking to satisfy in visions an idle desire for erudition in history or archeology. He has a nobler aim, that of the soul's sanctification, and to arouse in the individual a love of Jesus suffering. He is like a painter who, in order to excite our piety, is content to paint scenes in His own manner, but without departing too far from the truth.[7] What would be the use of seeing the exact costume that the various persons were wearing on that particular day? whether their garments were red or blue?

We have positive proof of these partial modifications. For some saints, beholding Jesus on the Cross, perceived that there were three nails only; others saw four. Consequently, it is clear that God has not chosen to decide this controverted question by a revelation.[8]

12. — God has another reason for modifying certain **details**. Sometimes He adds them to a historical scene in order to bring out the secret meaning of the mystery. The actual spectators saw nothing similar.

Catherine Emmerich believed Mary of Agreda to have taken literally a large number of pictures which she should have understood allegorically and spiritually (*Vie de Jésus Christ*, by Catherine Emmerich, Vol. I, Preface by Brentano, ch. ix).

13. — So, too, in visions of Paradise, Purgatory, or Hell, God only shows in part that reality which is so far beyond our powers of understanding. He adapts Himself to our nature by making use of **symbols**. The saints and angels show themselves to us with bodies, which they do not in reality possess; they are clothed in rich

garments, and take part in processions or ceremonies. Heaven becomes a banquet or an exquisite garden. These pictures appear in accordance with the ideas of the person who sees them, or those of the painters of his day. We have an example of this in St. Lidwine's vision (see *Vie*, by Huysmans, ch. viii), and in that of the Book of Revelation [4:6-8] of the four living creatures round about the Throne. St. John borrowed its chief features from Ezekiel [1:5-14], who himself took the imagery from the gigantic bas-relief of the Assyrian palaces which the Jews had ever before their eyes during the Babylonian captivity.

All this should be understood in a spiritual sense.

14. — These considerations will enable us to understand how Amort, who has made a deep study of these questions, was able to say: "The revelations of persons whose sanctity and doctrine have been approved by the doctors and heads of the Church, **contradict each other**; for example, those of St. Bridget, St. Gertrude, St. Catherine of Siena" (Part I, ch. xxii, 1, No. 24). He quotes Baronius as saying that St. Mechtildis and St. Bridget also contradict one another (Part I, ch. viii, No. 12).

15. — We see, therefore, that it is imprudent to seek to **remake history** by the help of the saints' revelations. Blessed Veronica of Binasco saw Our Lord's whole life pass before her eyes, as did also St. Frances of Rome and Catherine Emmerich. The Bollandists have reproduced her accounts of these visions (January 13), but they warn us in the preface (No. 4) that "learned men" consider that they contain many historical errors. The visions of St. Frances of Rome have been still more explicitly criticized. In the life written by Maria Anguillara, who succeeded the saint in the government of her Congregation of the Oblates in Rome, the authoress expresses herself with the following reserve: "*Many* of the things that she saw when in ecstasy must be considered as being merely *pious meditations* and contemplations *due to her own action*, especially those that concern Our Savior's Life and Passion; this is easily apparent in reading them. We cannot, however, deny that true revelations may

be mingled with them. Leaving the task of discrimination to the pious reader and to Superiors, I will, without distinction, transcribe all that the ancient manuscript contains" (Bolland., March 9, First *Life* of the saint; Preface, No. 10). The third cause of error would also apply here.

16. — *Third cause of error.* It may happen that during a vision the human mind retains the power of **mingling its action with the divine action** in a certain measure. We make a mistake, then, in attributing *purely* to God the information that is thus obtained. At times it is the memory that supplies its recollections; at others the inventive faculty that is at work.[9]

Various authors think that this danger is much to be feared when the person speaks during the ecstasy. For if he speaks, his sensible faculties have not completely lost their activity. They may then have a share in the revelation.

Amort considers this a proof that St. Frances of Rome was a factor in her own visions (see preceding number), for she was neither silent nor motionless in her ecstasies.

17. — There is a danger of confounding the divine action with our own, even in non-ecstatic prayer, when God seems to send us a somewhat strong **inspiration**. No matter how brief and almost instantaneous it may be, we like to think that it is longer, and the illusion is easy, for we do not know the precise moment when the divine influence ends and ours begins. When a stone is thrown into a calm lake, the shock only lasts for a moment, but the water does not immediately resume its former immobility. A series of ripples continues to rise from the spot, as if fresh stones were falling there. So in the soul, a movement once produced does not come suddenly to an end with the action that caused it. It seems as if we were continuing to receive something; but the notion is purely human.

18. — Further, those who often have true revelations may **become negligent** about discerning their origin, and they then prophesy falsely.

Saint Catherine Labouré, a Sister of Charity, who in November, 1830, received the revelation of the Miraculous Medal, foretold several events correctly (for instance, she announced forty years in advance, and with their exact date, the massacres of the Commune of 1870); but other predictions were not fulfilled. In such a case, so her biographer, M. Chevalier, tells us, she quietly acknowledged her mistake and would say, "Well, I have been mistaken; I thought that I was telling you correctly. I am very glad that the truth should be known."

19. — **What kind of** personal **ideas** are we specially inclined to attribute wrongly to divine influence, either during ecstasy or when in close union with God?

They consist of two kinds:

20. — 1° The ideas that **appeal to our own desires**. If we have a project greatly at heart, and still more if we are moved by the imprudent desire to see it encouraged by a revelation, it will easily seem to us that God is speaking in order to advise or command its execution.

21. — 2° **Preconceived ideas** in matters of *doctrine* or *history*, and also the recollection of anything that has struck us vividly in reading or conversation. Thus, when the person belongs to a religious congregation, his revelations are often colored by its doctrines. This is due to the ideas with which his mind is occupied, and also to the opinions of his Confessors. These latter act upon him unconsciously by their *repeated* instructions and by their manner of putting their questions, which lead naturally to certain answers, and sometimes more openly, by allowing it to be seen how much they desire that a revelation should come to stamp their ideas with approval.

The *Life* of St. Colette presents an example of the influence of these preconceived ideas. In accordance with the belief of her directors, she began by holding that St. Anne had been married three times and had had several daughters. She believed that she saw St.

Anne appear to her with all her supposed family (Bolland., May 25, p. 247, *Parergon*, No. 8).

Certain facts related in these disputed revelations are but reproductions of incidents belonging to the apocryphal gospels or legends of a later date. At the end of the Middle Ages and at the time of the Renaissance they were popularized by such books as James de Voragine's *Golden Legend.*

The errors that we have just enumerated have sometimes gone so far that it has been difficult to know how much value to attach to certain revelations made to the saints. Fr. Lancisius, quoted by Benedict XIV (*De Canon.*, Book III, ch. liii, No. 17; English trans., *Heroic Virtue*, Vol. III, ch. xiv, p. 404), says: "The revelations of some holy women [ecstatics] canonized by the Apostolic See, whose sayings and writings in rapture, and derived from rapture are *filled with errors*, are therefore not allowed to be published."

22. — As one of the principal causes of error is due to **the mental activity** of the person who has the revelation, it is as well to quote some examples of these cases.

23. — Let us begin with **St. Elizabeth**, the Benedictine Abbess **of Schoenau**, near Treves, and a friend of St. Hildegard (1129-65). She had many revelations on historical subjects, notably the martyrdom of St. Ursula and her companions, whose bones had just been discovered (1156). When these relics were brought to her she thought she knew supernaturally the names and the lives of those to whom they had belonged. To obtain more information, she plied her Guardian Angel and the saints with questions. At first she did not venture to do this; but her directors unfortunately encouraged her in this dangerous curiosity. And, further, the revelations having ceased, she caused the community to pray urgently for seventeen days that they might be continued (Bolland., June 18; *Life*, No. 102).

These were just the dispositions for being led astray. But the saint was persuaded, on the contrary, that all her revelations were the pure truth. She maintained this even on her deathbed, and was greatly astonished at encountering any opposition. She even went so far as to demand that they should be officially published during her lifetime. "I had just written the book of my revelations," she says, "when, on the feast of St. Peter and St. Paul, my Guardian Angel appeared to me and dictated these words for the Bishop of Treves, Cologne, and Mayence: 'Be it known from the great and terrible God and from me, the Angel of this book, that you are *to make known to the Holy Roman Church and to all the people* the words that are to be found in this work. Think not that they are women's tales! Almighty God is their author. What I say to you I say for *all*'" (*ibid.*, No. 106).

Posterity has not endorsed the saint's opinions. Amort proves that these visions are full of historical errors, and he attributes the greater part, at any rate, to imagination. The Bollandists have accepted his conclusions (October 21, Prologue to the *Life of St. Ursula*, 5).

24. — The Bollandists regard the revelations of **Blessed Hermann Joseph**, concerning St. Ursula, in the same light (*ibid.*, 7). But they do not for this reason dispute the other graces received by these two saints. They admit that Blessed Hermann prophesied truly and worked miracles.

25. — The study of the books written by **St. Hildegard** also shows us how human action can join itself to the divine action without our being aware of it. This saint must have received exceptional graces of infused knowledge and prophecy, otherwise we could not explain her influence upon her contemporaries.[10] She herself recognized, indeed, that this knowledge was not complete (see her works, published by Cardinal Pitra, p. 333). But she was convinced that she had added nothing of her own to it. This is what she wrote at the age of seventy: "I am *ignorant* of all that I do not see in my vision, for I am illiterate; and when I write by virtue of this light, I set down *no other words* than those that I have heard" (Migne ed., col. 18, A; Card. Pitra, p. 333).

And yet it is impossible to admit that all that this saint wrote came from God. For her works are full of scientific errors, and exactly those errors that were prevalent in the twelfth century.[11]

26. — We may then be allowed to think that God was content to **quicken her intelligence** and her imagination. In this state she was able to learn, to imagine, to remember in a far greater degree than would be possible in the normal state. But, unknown to her, much of her knowledge really proceeded from her frequent conversations with the theologians and learned men of her day, from books that she had read, or the sermons that she had heard.

It is very fortunate, let us add, that she was not in advance of the science of her time. If she had known the truths that have since been discovered in astronomy, physiology, and in physics, scientific men, instead of admiring, would have persecuted her, as has been the case with so many pioneers, and she would thus have lost a great part of her religious influence.

27. — In order to explain in a favorable light St. Hildegard's illusions on scientific subjects, we may admit the following **hypothesis:**

God, it seems, may supernaturally convey to a person's mind a portion of the knowledge of the day, such as it is found in existing books or in the minds of contemporary scientists; while giving in some way a general warning that He does not guarantee the contents of this whole, and that it is therefore to be accepted only at the receiver's risk.

Such a gift, although imperfect as regards certainty, would still be a magnificent one. Those among us who have toiled over our books during our whole lives, and who forget incessantly what we have learned, would be enchanted to possess such an expeditious process of learning and remembering.

The important point to remark is that God does not deceive the soul here, since, by our hypothesis, He has warned it in one way or another. God is satisfied with teaching supernaturally those things that the soul would have learned naturally. As regards certainty, the individual is no worse off than ordinary learned men.

Notwithstanding their confidence in their teachers, they admit that all science is subject to error, and that alongside of the solid and positive portions we find also some that are provisional and other that are falling into disrepute. If men fail to understand it aright, they have only their own want of cleverness, their mental inferiority, or their hastiness to blame.

28. — We will continue to give some examples, in spite of a very natural repugnance to discover either historic or scientific errors in saints whom we have delighted in regarding as infallible. But we must never be afraid of the truth. And, besides, the proofs that we give are useful: they justify the strict rules that we shall have to lay down later on upon the subject of revelations.

In St. Frances of Rome's time they believed in a sky composed of crystal. Imbued with this idea, she declares that she has seen it, seen it distinctly, in the numerous visions in which she visited the firmament. It is situated between the sky in which the stars are to be found and the empyrean. She compares these three skies as to light and beauty; her confessor having asked their relative distances one from the other, she said they were further one from another than the earth from the nearest sky. Not knowing that the blue of the sky is merely that of the atmosphere, she attributes it to the sky in which the stars were supposed to be, and which would consequently be a solid body (Bolland., March 9, First *Life*, No. 30).

29. — **St. Catherine of Ricci** was perhaps also influenced by preconceived ideas. All her life she had a great devotion for Savonarola, who was a friend of the family. She wished to rehabilitate the memory of the fiery tribune who strove to transform all Florence into a cloister, who plunged into political struggles and died at the stake in 1498. She strove to make him an object of public veneration as a prophet and martyr. He often appeared to her surrounded with glory and followed by his companions on the scaffold; he twice cured her suddenly of a serious illness. These appearances seemed an obstacle at first to Catherine's beatification. The *Promotor Fidei*,[12] the future Pope Benedict XIV, opposed it on this ground, declaring that the Sister had sinned in invoking a man whom the Church had handed over to the secular arm (*De Canon.*, Book III, ch. xxv, Nos. 17-20. English translation: Benedict XIV, *On Heroic Virtue*, Vol. I, ch. v, Nos. 17-20). This point was easily solved. But one more delicate still remained. To beatify Catherine, was not this to proclaim that these visions were divine? Now, according to these visions, Savonarola was a saint in the eyes of God, if not in those of men. A burning and controverted question had thus been decided by divine authority. Benedict XIII brought the discussion to a close by ordering Catherine's devotion to Savonarola, and consequently the apparitions which caused it, to be left out of the question (*ibid.*, and *Vie*, by P. Bayonne, Vol. II, ch. xvii. English *Life*, by F.M. Capes, pp. 270-271). This separating of the saint's virtues from visions amounted to a declaration of this principle: when a servant of God is canonized, it is his virtue that is canonized, and not his visions.

30. — Whatever opinion we may form as to **Mary of Agreda's** revelations, taken as a whole, we are obliged to admit that they contain some errors. Thus she fancied that she knew by revelation of the existence of a crystal sky (Part II, No. 17); that it was divided up into eleven portions at the moment of the Incarnation (*ibid.*, No. 128): this passage is omitted in the French translation. She learned that the six days of the Creation were each of twenty-four hours' duration[13]; that from the Fall to Our Lord's coming, there were 5199 years to a day. With regard to space, she says that the earth's radius is 1251 miles (Spanish). Amort has shown that these figures are false (*Observations*, prop. 2), like many others relating to dates and distances. He quotes twenty-one points on which she contradicts other revelations. Finally, she considers that it is a sin not to believe her (see Chapter Three, **27**). Now, this is a gross error. For the Church alone, and not any private revelation, has a right to impose belief on the faithful at large; and the Church imposes only such as are contained in Holy Scripture and tradition.

Theologians have pointed out other descriptions as being

probably the result of illusion. They are chiefly attributable to the desire to fill the Blessed Virgin's life with innumerable prodigies, showing a singular contrast to the simplicity of the gospels. We find in them all the pomp and splendor of the Spanish Court (see in the *Théologie mystique*, by Mgr. Chaillot, the censures passed upon this book at the Sorbonne and by Rome).

Let us not, however, conclude from this that Mary of Agreda deceived herself also as to her purely intellectual visions of the Divinity (*Cité mystique*, Part I, Book I, ch. ii). Amort, who has criticized her a great deal, begins by saying that, without doubt, "her virtues were heroic." "This stands out clearly," he says, "from her process of beatification which I read in Rome." He adds: "I unhesitatingly admit that she received wonderful lights from God; it is not likely that in her frequent raptures[14] so virtuous a person, whose death was without any features that could shock us, should have been constantly deceived by the Devil. But did not her imagination lead her astray, reproducing what she had read or heard about the Blessed Virgin, or what she had seen in theatrical performances? I leave the Church to be the judge on this matter" (Part II, No. XIII, prelude).

The eulogy just quoted will not appear exaggerated to those who read the life of the servant of God by Samaniégo. It is very beautiful, and gives the impression of great sanctity and a high degree of union with God.

With regard to her revelations, Amort remains doubtful. This seems the wisest attitude. For if many learned men, especially among the saint's fellow-countrymen, have been enthusiastic with regard to the *Mystical City*, others, no less numerous and learned, have refused it credence. They explain this book by the pious Sister's readings, combined with an exceptional power of invention, such as the great novelists have given us examples of (see Bossuet, *Remarques sur la mystique Cité*, at the end of Vol. XX, Lachat ed.). The psychology of Mary of Agreda, like that of St. Hildegard, is an enigma that we have not by any means completely solved. Clement XIV, of the Order of St. Francis, also showed that he regards her revelations as, to say the least, doubtful, since in his Decree of March 12, 1771, he forbids her Beatification to proceed "on account of the book" (see Mgr. Chaillot; conclusion).

Once more, it is a question only of Sister Mary's revelations. Let us beware of thinking that, if they are false, it is the same with her sanctity and her extraordinary union with God.

30 *bis.* — Alain de la Roche, a Breton Dominican (1428-75), is honored in his Order on September 8 with the title of Blessed. After teaching theology, he spent the last five years of his life in successfully instituting and propagating Confraternities of the Rosary in the north of France and in the Low Countries. He is not said to have had ecstasies, but he believed himself to have received many revelations, particularly of a historical kind. They served as the theme of his preachings on the Rosary. Shortly after his death, the Carthusians of Gripsholm, in Sweden, published the manuscript containing the chief of these discourses (*Sponsus novellus Beatissimae Virginis Mariae*, 1498). After protestations from Fathers Quétif and Echard (*Scriptores ordinis praedicatorum*, Vol. I, p. 851) and from the Bollandist, Cuper (1733), the majority of writers, even those of the Order of St. Dominic, agreed in regarding these revelations as being of no value. "He was undoubtedly a religious of sincere piety, but one who was led by a feverish imagination to strange hallucinations" (*Analecta Bollandiana*, 1903, p. 219). Alain believed firmly in his revelations: "All these things," he said, "I affirm them and bear witness to them on oath, by my faith in the Blessed Trinity. May I be accursed if I have departed from the way of truth!"

31. — *Fourth cause of error.* A true revelation may **subsequently be altered** involuntarily by the person who receives it.

This danger is to be feared with intellectual locutions. After receiving them, the temptation to translate them into words cannot be resisted; but there is the risk of slightly modifying the meaning of the thought, and particularly of giving it a precision that it lacked. Suppose that someone speaks to you simply by signs — by a movement of the eye, for instance — you would understand. But if you try to translate the intention by words, you risk adding shades of your own invention.

Thus when praying for one who is sick, you may receive an assurance of a cure; but God leaves you in ignorance as to whether it will be total or partial, sudden or slow, soon or late, or even physical or moral. It is difficult to translate this communication without making it more definite than it was originally.

32. — The danger is also great when the written **revelation** is very long and yet has been received almost **instantaneously**. It is not rash to believe that not all the words used were supplied by the revelation, and that the thoughts were not given in detail. They were developed later by the person who received them.

St. Bridget recognizes that this is sometimes so in her own case. In fact, in one of her visions Our Lord, without blaming her, remarks that she retouches her revelations, through not having understood them properly, or not knowing how to express them exactly (*nunc volvis et* revolvis *in animo tuo, nunc scribis et* rescribis *ea, donec veneris ad proprium sensum verborum meorum. Revelationes Extravagantes*, ch. xlix); and, further, He approves the saint's secretaries who in translating from Swedish into Latin add "color and ornamentation."

33. — *Fifth cause of error.* I have just referred to **secretaries.** They may easily alter the text without any wrong intention, for their own personality intervenes in the choice of expressions. They sometimes, with a certain amount of good faith, think that they can add whole sentences under pretext of making the thought clearer. "We know (they say to themselves) that this is what the saint wished to say." The account gains perhaps in clarity; but only half of it is revelation.

We have examples of these cases where the accuracy of the text is disputed: those of Mary of Agreda, Catherine Emmerich and Marie Lataste. We may read them for edification but we do not know exactly in what measure their revelations, even supposing them to have been true originally, have been retouched.[15] Many persons believe these writings to be a mixture. There would have been three concurrent actions: the divine revelation, the seer's own activity (which has interpreted or invented and perhaps supplied a good half of the results), finally the embellishments made by secretaries and friends.

Benedict XIV (*De Canon.*, Book III, ch. liii, No. 16; English: *On Heroic Virtue*, Vol. III, ch. ix, No. 16) examines one of St. Catherine of Siena's celebrated revelations (ecstasy of 1377), in which the Blessed Virgin would practically have told her that she was not immaculate. He quotes several authors who for the sake of the saint's reputation prefer to sacrifice that of her directors or editors who are thus accused of falsification. He afterwards gives us Fr. Lancisius' opinion admitting the possibility of the saint having deceived herself as a result of preconceived ideas (*ibid.*, No. 17; Lancisius opusc. *De praxi divinae praesentiae*, ch. xiii).[16]

34. — **Compilers**, like secretaries have sometimes modified revelations. Thus in the first German edition of Catherine Emmerich's works it was said that St. James the greater was present at the Blessed Virgin's death. It was afterwards seen that this statement was incompatible with the chronology of events in the Acts of the Apostles. In the recent Ratisbon edition the erroneous phrase has simply been effaced. This method is deplorable for it robs the serious reader of a means of forming his opinions. The sentence should have been retained adding a note saying: the Sister was mistaken here. Are they afraid lest this avowal should interfere with the sale of the book?

Fr. Croset, who translated Mary of Agreda in the seventeenth century, softened down certain passages. I am told that in an edition that appeared at the end of the nineteenth century the style of this translation has again been retouched, making fresh suppressions.

2. *Five causes of absolutely false revelations*

35. — These five causes are: 1° Simulation; 2° an over lively mind or imagination; 3° an illusion of the memory that consists in believing that we recall certain facts which never happened; 4° the Devil's action; 5° the inventions of falsifiers.

36. — *First cause of falseness.* To begin with, it may happen that the persons who claim to have received these revelations are **untruthful** and in bad faith. One of the best known examples is Magdalen of the Cross, a Franciscan of Cordova, who lived at the beginning of the sixteenth century.

She was born in 1487, entered the Convent at the age of seventeen, in 1504, and was three times Abbess of her Monastery. From the age of five the Devil appeared to her under the form of different saints, and inspired her with a strong desire to pass as a saint herself. She was thirteen when he considered that her soul was sufficiently possessed by the spirits of vanity, pride, and sensuality; he plainly declared his identity to her, and promised that if she would enter into an agreement with him, he would spread abroad her reputation for sanctity and would procure her, for thirty years at the least, all the pleasures that she desired. She agreed, and Satan became her councillor, although there were days when she would gladly have driven him away, so terrified was she at the fearful shapes that he took. Thanks to his aid, she realized all the outward appearance of divine marvels: ecstasies, levitation, predictions that were often fulfilled. She made herself the stigmatic wounds, and for eleven years persuaded others that she lived without taking any food; while procuring it for herself secretly. For thirty-eight years, up to 1543, she succeeded in deliberately deceiving the greatest theologians in Spain, the Bishops, Cardinals, Inquisitors, and great nobles about the Court. People came from all sides to consult her, and alms were showered upon her. Having been at death's door, she confessed everything publicly, and then regretted her avowals. Exorcism had to be resorted to before the Devil lost his hold over her will. Finally, she was condemned to be confined in another Convent of her Order (Amort, Book II, ch. iii; Görres, Vol. V, ch. xi; Bizouard, Vol. II, Book X, ch. iv; Dr. Imbert, Vol. II, p. 1).

36 *bis.* — Mgr. Dupanloup, Bishop of Orleans, in a letter to one of his clergy, March 23, 1874, says: "Cardinal Albitius, who wrote about the middle of the seventeenth century, enumerates in his great work *de Inconstantia in fide* more than twenty condemnations pronounced in his time" by the Holy Office against simulators. He adds that in 1747 a professed religious of the monastery of St. Clare, at Chieri, was condemned for the same reason; also, under Pius VII, one named Jeanne Marella (simulated stigmata); and in 1857, a certain Catherine Finelli (Letter published in *Le Correspondant*, March 25, 1874, p. 1105).

37. — *Second cause of falseness.* We will now suppose a person who is in good faith. He may perhaps be deceived by his **imagination** or his **mind**, that are **over lively**. It was said above (**16**) that our faculties sometimes mingle their own action with the divine revelation. But, when the temperament is badly balanced or over-excited, they may do still more: they construct an altogether false revelation. Thanks to their feverish imaginations, such persons, during the most ordinary prayer, can pronounce interior words with such distinctness that they seem to be said by someone else.

Or, again, on particular days they have an extraordinary power of visual representation. A picture offers itself to their interior eyes with very vivid colors, almost equal to those shown by real objects. If a scene of Our Lord's life is in question, or some future event in which they are interested, they willingly believe that the picture is supernatural.

There are even cases where the illusion may take the form of thinking that an intellectual vision of a saint has been seen. This is when it is obscure. For instance, you imagine, without any sufficient reason, that you feel the saint near you. It is necessary to be much more exacting as regards proof here than when it is a question of the presence of God. With regard to God, the error does

not go to the lengths of affirming a presence that does not exist —
He is there; the question is simply that of knowing if He makes
Himself felt. It is quite otherwise with the saints.

The same must be said with regard to intellectual locutions.
This is how St. John of the Cross speaks of them: "There are some
men whose intellect is so quick and penetrating that their concep-
tions, when they are self-recollected, naturally proceed with great
facility, and form themselves into these locutions and reasonings
so clearly [it is a question of intellectual locutions, as was stated in
a preceding chapter, the twenty-third] as to make them think that
God is speaking. But it is not so. All this is the work of the intellect, somewhat *disengaged from the operations of sense*, for it may do
this and even more *without any supernatural help whatever*, by its
own natural light. This is a state of things of frequent occurrence,
and many delude themselves into the belief that… God converses
with them: they write down, or cause others to write for them, what
they have experienced. And, after all, it is nothing" (*Ascent of Mount
Carmel*, Book II, ch. xxix, p. 192).

St. Teresa, it is true, says that when a person has had true visions or true locutions they can no longer be confused with the
feeble imitations of the imagination. But for those who have never
had experience of these divine favors the difficulty continues
undiminished.[17]

38. — It may happen that this imaginative power has an accidental cause. Cardinal Bona says that hallucinations may at times
result from excessive abstinences, **fasts** and vigils; this excess en-
feebles the muscular system and the faculties; they cause a predomi-
nance of the nervous system (*De discret. spir.*, ch. xx, No. 3).
Benedict XIV adopts this view (*De Canon.*, Book III, ch. 1, No. 1;
On Heroic Virtue, Vol. III, ch. xii, No. 1).

39. — *Third cause of falseness.* This is an **illusion** or special
disease of the memory, which consists in thinking that certain facts
are remembered, although they never existed.

This illusion would seem impossible, and yet it is seen even outside mystic things: certain minds invent stories and sincerely persuade themselves that the incidents occurred. These are *inventors in good faith*. This case must not be confused with the preceding, where the imagination *conjures up a picture*, nor with another, much more common, that of romancers who relate imaginary anecdotes, *as a joke*, and finish by being half persuaded of their historic origin. Those that I am now speaking of are earnest persons who invent right and left, but *who believe what they say*, and this from the first moment of saying it.

Some will relate their journeys in distant countries where their friends know quite well that they have never been. They describe the least details, which are always picturesque. Others believe that they have visited Kings, Bishops or other prominent personages, who have confided to them secrets or important opinions, or who have encouraged them warmly. Finally, others describe the fearful dangers that they have escaped, or the unworthy persecutions of which they have been the object.[18] We are disposed to believe them, for their tone is one of such conviction; and then they enter into details with regard to time and locality and the conversations that took place, until we say to ourselves: It is impossible that the foundation of all this should not be true. And yet all is invented.

These people are not mad; in all other things they are reasonable and intelligent, although usually in a state of agitation and excitement. How are we to explain their aberration? We do not know. But there is a strange confusion between the *imagination*, which constructs a scene, and the *memory*, which affirms that it took place. The reason no longer distinguishes between these two very different operations. They probably begin by thinking of the anecdote as possible in itself, then as possible for themselves, then as likely, then as probable, then as certain. It is after this unconscious elaboration, and when the illusion has come to its full maturity, that they relate the history to us.

Let us not endeavor to explain this illusion, which is fairly common. Let us simply apply it to our subject. Let us imagine, for example, certain persons who, leading a very retired life, have the unfortunate turn of mind which I have just described. They will not be inclined to lay claim to long voyages, or dinners with political or literary celebrities. This would be too much; they have still enough good sense to understand that people would laugh in their faces. They will rather invent facts that cannot be disproved. An exalted piety will sometimes incline them to the side of revelations. They relate that they were visited by the Court of Heaven, and that Our Lady herself gave them her salutary counsels. If they have the "passion for persecutions," they may invent or exaggerate those which they suffer from men or devils.

The director will always find that his advice has little effect; which will be a first means of unmasking the illusion. There is yet another: that of informing himself as to these persons' lives as a whole. If they have the defect of always exaggerating, they will show it in many other circumstances. It will occasionally take some time to arrive at a clear view of the situation. But where is the need of hurry?

40. — *Fourth cause of falseness.* The Devil may give false revelations or visions. His action may *sometimes* be recognized by the circumstances of the vision (see the following chapter).

He can also produce alienation of the sensible faculties, trying to counterfeit the divine ecstasy. This case must be extremely rare, for hardly any undoubted examples are quoted. I have cited (**36**) that of Magdalen of the Cross; but here it was a purely exterior imitation, and made in complicity with the person involved.

In the seventeenth century there was an example of the Devil's action upon a young woman, Nicole of Reims, who seems to have been in good faith. André du Val gives her story at great length in Mme. Acarie's *Life* (Book I, ch. vi). Nicole appeared to possess the most extraordinary graces; she was approved and consulted by a number of pious persons; she even seemed to labor for the conversion of souls; she organized public prayers and processions. Mme. Acarie was alone in affirming that it was all due to the Devil. At last one day the young woman reverted to her natural state so completely "that she no longer had this sublime turn of mind, these beautiful discourses... nor the appearance of these great virtues. She was very coarse, rough, and imperfect.... She married, and was on the point of becoming a Huguenot."

41. — *Fifth cause of falseness.* The inventions of falsifiers.

Political prophecies have often been their handiwork. They were inspired by motives of political or pecuniary interest, or by the desire to mystify the public.

We find an instance of the first motive at the time of the taking of Constantinople by the Turks (1453). The future schismatic Patriarch, Georges Scholarios, who was secretly on their side, through hatred of the Latins, wished to dishearten the defenders of the city. With this object, and he afterwards admitted this himself, he composed false prophecies, upon which the people fed eagerly. One of these predictions announced that the assailants would begin by entering the city, but would suddenly be miraculously routed.

At other times the authors simply wished to amuse themselves at the expense of credulous persons. A prophecy made by Cazotte, on the subject of the French Revolution, has often been reprinted. But now it is thought to have been composed after the event by La Harpe. It may have had a historical foundation, but a less marvellous one than it was made out to be. Suppose that the death of Louis XVI and the French Revolution were really foretold. These events were decided beforehand by secret societies; Cazotte, who was a high dignitary among the German *illuminati*, knew these projects and could easily foretell their fulfillment.

Another famous prophecy is that of Orval; it was made in 1839 and was supposed to have been found in a book printed in the fifteenth century. It contains minute details relating to events of a date previous to the year of its publication. The rest is obscure. The Bishop of Verdun, in a circular letter of February 6, 1849, declares that the author was a priest of his diocese. "In the beginning," the Bishop says, "he had no object in this fraud other than

an aimless amusement; but when time brought about the fulfillment of some of his predictions, vanity on the one hand, and false
shame on the other, caused him to persevere in a course of action
from which he was afterwards glad to escape." (This letter is quoted
intact at the end of Fr. Pouplard's book, *Un mot sur les visions*).

Later writers, such as the Abbé Curicque (*Voix prophétiques*),
have disputed the genuineness of the foregoing confession, saying
that it was wrung from him by intimidation, and they quote witnesses who stated that they had read a *similar* prophecy at the time
of the Revolution. As no authentic copy of such a prophecy has
been preserved, no one can say how far this resemblance goes. But
even if the editor of 1839 embellished an ancient document, it is
none the less true that he was a falsifier of facts.

42. — The different causes of falseness just enumerated have
often been combined with the object of giving publicity to false
prophecies of a political nature. These abound particularly at times
of great **political or religious upheaval**, the popular imagination
being then overexcited.

In the thirteenth century St. Bonaventure complained of hearing "to satiety" prophecies dealing with the Church's troubles and
the end of the world (*De profectu religiosorum*, Book III, ch. lxxvi).

At the end of the fourteenth century, during the great Western Schism, "seers arose on all sides, and their visions gained such
an influence and a circulation as had been unknown before…. In
some of the gravest sermons reliance was put upon these baseless
predictions" (Salambier, *The Great Schism of the West*, ch. vi, 4).
Gerson, who took part in the Council of Constance, at which the
Great Schism and the struggle between the rival Popes was put an
end to, says that there were then an incredible number of *holy and
mortified* men who had false revelations at this period, and that he
has this information from credible witnesses. He adds: "Many believed that they had learned by revelation and with certainty that
they would themselves be the future Pope" (*De distinctione verarum
visionem*).

At the beginning of the sixteenth century Italy experienced a regular epidemic of politico-religious prophecies. This effervescence began with those made by Savonarola in Florence. Religious and hermits swarmed over the country, and while commenting upon the Book of Revelation, they announced from the pulpit or in public places revolutions in the temporal and spiritual governments, to be followed by the end of the world. Peasants and young girls alike fell to prophesying.

In the fifth Lateran Council, in 1516, Leo X was obliged to publish a Bull by which public prophecies by preachers were prohibited (Pastor, *History of the Popes*, edited by Fr. Antrobus, Vol. V, end of *Introduction*; also Mansi, Collection of Councils).

Let us now come to the eighteenth century. There were "prophecies springing up constantly during the French Revolution, prophecies that were clear and full of detail with regard to past events, vaguer as to future occurrences and often refuted by facts when they thought fit to be definite; promising a deliverer who did not appear, and soon substituting another prediction, which was put forward in the character of an infallible utterance" (Abbé Sicard, *L'ancien Clergé de France*, Vol. III, Book III, ch. vi, p. 153).

In the nineteenth century we have also epidemics of prophesyings: they announced the Comte de Chambord's reign, or that of the Naundorff. They took their inspiration from doubtful prophecies regarding "the great Pope and the great King," which the Ven. Holzhauser had inserted in his *Commentary on the Apocalypse* in the seventeenth century. It is to be regretted that religious journals should so often have collected and spread abroad these absurdities which bring religion into discredit.

In a letter already quoted (**36** *bis*), Mgr. Dupanloup laments the great number of prophecies "that are hawked about on all sides by the enterprise of booksellers." "I have now," he says, "more than twenty volumes before me, from Belgium and France in particular" (p. 1108). He recalls the words of Pius IX in his allocution of April 9, 1872: "I do not give much credit to prophecies, because those especially that have recently appeared do not merit the honor of being read"; and this other, of July 5, 1872: "A large number of prophecies are in circulation; but I think that they are the fruit of the imagination."

The twentieth century is in no wise behind its predecessors. When, in 1901, the French Chambers were discussing at great length the laws that were destined to destroy the Religious Orders, prophetic imaginations came into play. Certain visionaries felt themselves impelled to go to the Holy Father to confide to him their predictions and secrets. One of their directors told me that on arriving in Rome his penitent was much surprised to find ten other persons who had come with the same intention. A cardinal listened to them very patiently, but audience with the Holy Father was refused to them. I have it from a reliable source that one of the present claimants to the French throne constantly receives letters from prophets and prophetesses who foretell his destinies and give him advice, professedly in God's name. He is weary of them.

43. — Nothing is easier than to invent **political prophecies** in this way. It is only necessary to announce the advent of great misfortunes to be followed by extraordinary deliverances. These statements can be put about without fear, for no one can prove the contrary.

A suspicious character in *modern* political prophecies is the fact that they never lead us to withstand wicked men, and never suggest any serious manner of resisting them. Some even predict that the world is to change suddenly, *by a miracle.* "A new era" is on the point of appearing; everyone will become holy in an instant. The conclusion drawn from such predictions is that we should fold our arms and wait. Since God is to do everything, and makes a point of proclaiming it in advance, it would be an indiscretion and foolishness on our part to wish to help Him and to anticipate His appointed hour. Let us, then, go on doing nothing! This is a convenient doctrine.

I was objecting to one of these false prophetesses, one day, that the world seems, on the contrary, to become more and more wicked, and that we were proceeding in the opposite direction to the great renovation that she was announcing. She replied: "It is a good sign. God will not intervene until the evil is at its height." This answer teaches us nothing. When can anyone say that the evil is at its height? And, further, you declare that this maximum will be reached soon, and not in two thousand years. How do you know this?

---

3. The security of the mystic union, as compared with revelations

44. — We have just seen that **revelations** are subject to many illusions. Our own action, especially, may counterfeit the divine action, or mingle with it. This first drawback brings with it others still more grave. In fact, the revelations do not generally aim at being useful to the seer's own soul only; they lead to exterior acts, such as the teaching of a doctrine, the propagation of a devotion, prophesying, or embarking on some enterprise that requires considerable expense. If these impulses came from God, and from Him alone, no evil results could be feared. But in the contrary case, which is much more frequent and difficult to discover, the soul begins to tread in perilous paths. Hence it follows that revelations are usually a source of danger.

45. — On the other hand, with the **mystic union** there is nothing to fear. We will put things at their worst, and suppose that the state of prayer is nothing but a pure imitation. From the moment that this prayer claims resemblance with the mystic state and cannot be distinguished from it with any certainty, it is that it presents the same characteristics and, in particular, that it inclines the soul to divine love and the practice of the virtues. This result is excellent. Further, it does not lead to the exterior acts enumerated above, otherwise it would degenerate into revelation, which is contrary to the hypothesis. And thus it is *completely inoffensive*. And, moreover, I have made too great a concession. I have supposed that

the mystic state could be counterfeited by the human mind or by the Devil. I have shown the contrary elsewhere. Therefore a state of prayer, which in all seriousness presents the general aspects of the mystic state, comes from God, and cannot thus be other than advantageous.

46. — Mysticism is so little studied, even in many religious Houses, that numbers of pious persons confound revelations with the mystic union, or are, at least, unaware that these should be **appreciated differently**. They accordingly fall into one of the two following exaggerations:

1° If they are acquainted with the *danger of revelations*, they extend their adverse judgment to the mystic union and turn certain souls away from an excellent path.

2° If, on the contrary, they are persuaded, and rightly so, of the *security and utility of the mystic union*, they wrongly include revelations in this favorable verdict, and urge certain souls into a dangerous way.

Notes

---

[1] The servants of God of whom I shall speak, trying sometimes to find a favorable explanation of the facts related, number thirty-two. I give them in alphabetical order: Blessed Alain de la Roche, Blessed Amadeus, Sister Andriveau, Blessed Bonomi, St. Bridget, St. Catherine of Bologna, St. Catherine of Ricci, St. Catherine of Siena, Catherine Emmerich, St. Colette, St. Elizabeth of Schoenau, St. Frances of Rome, St. Gertrude, Sister Gojoz, Blessed Hermann Joseph, St. Hildegard, Ven. Holzhauser, St. Joan of Arc, the Prophet Jonah, Blessed Jordan of Saxony, Saint Anne-Catherine Labouré, Marie Lataste, Ven. Mary of Agreda, Ven. Marina de Escobar, St. Mechtildis, Mélanie of La Salette, St. Monica, St. Norbert, St. Peter, Blessed Veronica of Binasco, St. Vincent Ferrer, Blessed Anna-Maria Taigi.

[2] Let us not say, "Out of respect for the saints, it is better to conceal the few illusions from which they may have suffered." Leo XIII, on the contrary, was not afraid to remind historians of Cicero's motto: "Speak nothing that is false; be silent regarding nothing that is true" (*ne quid falsi dicere audeat; ne quid veri non audeat*. Brief *Saepe numero*, August 18, 1883).

[3] I need not enter carefully here into the question of what should be thought of certain books of revelations, taken as a whole, that have had a great reputation, such as

those of Mary of Agreda, Catherine Emmerich, etc. A treatise on mysticism should keep to general principles, illustrated by certain examples. Their application to a whole book is a subject for a special treatise.

[4] See *La Vraie Jeanne d'Arc*, by P. Ayrolles, Vol. II, ch. v, No. 4, p. 161; or the *Procès de Jeanne d'Arc*, by Jules Quicherat, Vol. I, March 14.

[5] He supplemented this revelation by his own reasonings, with which he did not confuse it. "I have formed an opinion and a belief of *great probability* in my own mind, but *without sufficient certainty* to preach it, that Antichrist was born nine years ago."

[6] See *Histoire* of the saint by Fr. Fages, O.P. (Paris: Picard, 1901). It contains many references and facts. The author sums up his discussion of the prophecy of the Last Judgment in these words: "The preaching of Jonah saved Nineveh, that of Vincent Ferrer saved the world."

[7] This argument cannot be applied to the historical books of the Bible. For God has proposed to preserve certain facts of religious history for our instruction there. But we have no proof that He had a similar aim in the visions of the ecstatics. Their contradictory statements actually prove the contrary in many cases.

[8] In the first category were St. Mary Magdalen of Pazzi, Blessed Varani, Blessed Gerardesca of Pisa, and Catherine Emmerich. St. Clare of Montefalco and St. Veronica Giuliani had the three nails imprinted on their hearts. The second category is represented by St. Bridget. There is even a difference with regard to the form of the Cross, and whether it was set up before or after the Crucifixion (see the Bollandists, May 25, p. 246; *Parergon*, No. 2).

Certain stigmatics have had the wound on the shoulder; but with some it has been on the right, and with others on the left. And the same with the wound in the side (Dr. Imbert, Vol. II, ch. vi, p. 77).

There are other historical contradictions occurring in well-known visions, which I still avoid discussing as a whole. Catherine Emmerich says that Our Lady died thirteen years after her Son (*Life of the Blessed Virgin*, Part II, ch. xii). Sister Gojoz gives the same figures (*Vie*, by Mère de Provane, Part III, ch. viii); Mary of Agreda reckons twenty-one years, four months, and nineteen days (*Cité mystique*, Part III, Book VIII, ch. xix); St. Bridget, fifteen years (Book VII, ch. xxvi); St. Elizabeth of Schoenau, a year and a half (Bolland., June 18, No. 110). The third said that Mary was raised from the dead three days after her death (*ibid.*, ch. xxi); the fourth, fifteen days; the fifth, forty days; Blessed Bonomi says three days.

St. Bridget (Book VII, ch. xxi) and Mary of Agreda (Part II, Nos. 479, 481) contradict each other with regard to the Nativity at Bethlehem. There and elsewhere they both enter into details that are quite useless and which pious souls could no longer tolerate.

[9] Fr. Séraphin has written a volume in vindication of Mary of Agreda. The force of his argument loses considerably from the fact that, *without being aware of it*, he bases it upon the false principle that a non-diabolic revelation is *entirely* divine or *entirely* human. He also believes that the mind can contribute nothing to intellectual visions (p. 173), which is not always true (see 37).

[10] She never learned to read or to write, and neither music nor Latin. She acquired all these things miraculously: and she also understood the meaning of the Bible and the writings of the "philosopher-saints" (Migne ed., col. 104, A.). Another proof of a supernatural intervention regarding her knowledge of Latin is that she grasped, as

a whole, the sense of the passages that she was reading, without being able to separate the different words or parse the cases and tenses (Migne, col. 384, A). She needed a secretary to correct what she dictated in this language.

She had no ecstasies (Cardinal Pitra, *loc. cit.*). She derived her knowledge from a divine light which she received uninterruptedly from the age of three, and this when she was awake (Migne, col. 384, A; 13, D). She called it the shadow of the living light. From time to time she received a still higher knowledge, that of God; and she called this, by contrast, the living light (Migne, col. 18, A). Mary of Agreda gives us a similar description of her knowledge (*Cité mystique*, Part I, Book I, ch. ii).

This enlightenment with regard to created things and events had a special character in the case of Blessed Anna-Maria Taigi (1769-1837). For forty-seven years she saw close to her a symbolic sun which seemed to be as large as the natural sun. When she looked at it (she did not allow herself to do so without a motive) she saw many things that were useful for souls. These were often arranged around the sun, as though in some living picture. She was thus enabled to answer questions promptly and accurately, and almost without giving time to have the subject explained to her. Is this to say that she never made a mistake? The process of her beatification will show us. She predicted a great temporal triumph for the Church in terms that led her friends, and Pius IX himself, to believe that it would be realized under this Pontiff. Nothing of the sort occurred.

[11] One of her writings in particular is full of errors. This is *The Book of the Subtilties of Nature*, a treatise on physics and medicine, in nine books and 534 chapters (Migne, col. 1126), where the qualities of physical bodies are explained after the ancient methods, by the (purely fanciful) proportions in which they contain dryness and humidity, heat and cold. See especially the chapters on the air, the sapphire, the lodestone, eggs, the mandrake, the basilisk, the elephant, the lion, the dragon (which she believes in and describes without any hesitation), the unicorn, the griffin, etc. See also the *Liber divinorum operum*, visions 3 and 4, where the saint shows in 124 chapters the relation that appears to her to exist between the spiritual world and those of astronomy and physiology.

She also attributed to a supernatural source the music that she composed, and the new and strange language, a dictionary of which she compiled. No one has been able to discover its utility; which proves that it was probably merely the product of her own imagination. She seems to have had exceptional graces and great illusions.

[12] Popularly known as the Devil's Advocate [Translator].

[13] She even lays down that the Angels were created on the first day, "which answers to the Sunday"; they were cast out of Heaven on Monday morning and conspired until Thursday morning (Part I, No. 122); Adam was created very early on Friday morning, March 25 (Part II, No. 138).

[14] These ecstasies presented some extraordinary characteristics: 1° She came out of them immediately when one of her Superiors gave her the order mentally and from a distance; 2° she was usually raised above the ground. Her fellow Religious yielded at last to the curiosity displayed by strangers, and after the Communion they opened the Choir grate so that she could be easily seen. "They removed the veil that covered her face, so that her extraordinary beauty could be seen, and these lay persons used to make the experiment of seeing her move by merely blowing on her from outside the grate.... They advised that nothing of this should be told the servant of God" (*Life* by Samaniégo, ch. xiii). But, finally at the end of three or four years she

came to know of it by chance. She tried to avoid this publicity by going to make her thanksgiving in a room, the key of which she turned in the door. But the nuns removed some of the planks of a partition; they conveyed her through the opening, "carrying her easily as though she were a feather" (*ibid.*). The pious Sister was finally told about this. Seized with horror, she prayed that God would take away everything that was visible outwardly. She was then twenty-two years of age. Her prayer was granted. For the remaining forty years of her life her interior graces had no further effect upon her body. The other Sisters were dissatisfied at first by this change, and their explanations were of an unfavorable nature. But four years later they elected her Abbess. It was during this hidden time that she had her revelations on the Blessed Virgin's life.

[15] When Marie Lataste's *Works* appeared, the theologians, who had admired certain passages, ended by proving that they had been translated word for word from St. Thomas' *Summa*. They counted thirty-two passages of this nature. This objection was conveyed to the person who was supposed to have collected the revelations. He did not deny the fact, but replied majestically that, as Our Lord had inspired St. Thomas to write these pages, He could repeat them to Marie Lataste! Circumstances pointed, however, to a simpler explanation, which subsequent events tended to confirm.

Catherine Emmerich had a symbolic vision showing that Mary of Agreda's *Works* had been recast and amplified (Preface by Brentano, already quoted). Who is right in this disagreement?

[16] In the archives of the Generals of the Dominican Order there is a manuscript dating from 1398 which contains this relation (Book of Prayers, prayer 16).

[17] St. Teresa: "Not three or four only, but a large number of people have spoken to me on the subject, and therefore *I know by experience* that there are souls which, either because they possess vivid imaginations or active minds, are so wrapped up in their own ideas as to feel certain they see whatever their fancy imagines. *If they had ever beheld a genuine vision*, they would recognize the deception *at once*. They themselves fabricate, piece by piece, what they fancy they see: — *no aftereffects are produced* on the mind, which is left *less moved to devotion* than by the sight of a sacred picture" (*Interior Castle*, Sixth Mansion, ch. ix, 6). The saint reverts to the same idea, *ibid.*, 6, ch. iii, and three times in ch. xxv of her *Life*.

[18] At times their faculty for invention will have more unfortunate results: they will carry their calumnies to the point of denunciation. The Law Courts have had to decide cases where serious accusations have been brought, *with full conviction* and all the appearances of probability, against doctors or priests and the *impossibility* of the facts alleged have been proved. If I leave the subject of mysticism for a moment in order to speak of this tendency, it is for the sake of putting people on their guard against certain accusations. It is necessary to acquaint ourselves not only with the story, but with the narrator.

CHAPTER THREE

COURSE TO BE FOLLOWED IN OUR JUDGMENTS WITH REGARD TO THEM

---

1. Of the degree of probability or certainty that can be arrived at

1. — Let us first consider this question: Can we ever be morally certain that a revelation is *purely* divine?

Yes; although when we think of all the causes of error that have been enumerated it would not appear to be so.

2. — And first, when He so wills, God can give a complete certainty, while the revelation lasts, at any rate, to the person **receiving it**. The light and the *evidence* are of such strength that any kind of doubt is impossible.

A similar fact occurs in the natural order. Our senses are subject to many illusions. But it is none the less true that in a multitude of cases we feel that we cannot have been mistaken.

3. — Can we ever be certain that a **revelation made to another person** is purely divine?

Yes. For the Old Testament prophets furnished *indubitable* signs of their mission. Otherwise they would not have been believed, and, further, it would not have been right to believe them. For there were always false prophets who obtained a hearing from a section of the people and led them astray. Holy Scripture enjoined discernment in the matter.

By what means can this result be obtained? That is the important but difficult question with which we shall deal in this chapter.

4. — When a **miracle**[1] is performed, and it is stated that it is worked with this intention, or when circumstances show this to be the case, it is an undeniable proof of the divine nature of the revelation. A prophecy fulfilled, will be the equivalent of a miracle if it was couched in definite language and could not have been the result of chance or a conjecture of the Devil.

Apart from these rather rare means of forming an opinion, there is another which is slower and more delicate: the *discussion* of reasons for and against.

5. — This inquiry, in practice, usually gives nothing more than a greater or a lesser **probability**. And when this is so we must not be afraid to own it.

Authors are often satisfied with vague utterances on these questions. They certainly speak of *signs* of discernment; but they forget to point out that, taken separately, these signs do not furnish a complete certainty and that their existence is not always easily detected.

In the same way they speak of divine action, but they do not always ask themselves whether this divine action is absolutely without any admixture of another element. And yet this is an important point also.

6. — **The right course to adopt**, when judging revelations or visions, can be summed up in the three following steps which I am about to examine separately: 1° Obtain detailed information regarding **the person** who thinks himself thus favored; 2° and also as to the actual facts of the revelation; 3° these data once obtained, draw the *conclusions* that they indicate.

In order to show that a revelation is divine, *the process of exclusion* is also resorted to at times. This consists in proving that neither the Devil nor the individual mind can have added their own activity to God's action, and that no one retouched the revelation afterwards. But this process differs from the preceding one only by the manner of classifying the information and drawing the conclusions. Practically the same inquiries have to be made, but in a less natural order.

6 *bis.* — Theologians, as such, have the following **problem** only to solve with regard to visions and revelations: *Is this state purely divine, or is it not?* It is only indirectly, and as a means of solution, that they will ask themselves this other, slightly different question: *Is this state purely natural, or is it not?*

This second problem is often as difficult as the first. Psychology cannot yet furnish definite replies concerning certain supernormal operations of the human mind, such as those observed in hypnotism, somnambulism, telepathy, thought-reading, experiments with mediums, etc. With regard to these obscure facts we must maintain a very reserved attitude. In such matters we should pronounce in favor of the existence of the supernatural in simple and evident cases only.

---

2. *Seven kinds of inquiries to be made regarding the person who believes himself to be thus favored*

---

7. — Before examining the text or the circumstances of a revelation, we must know **with whom we have to deal**. There is a series of questions for this purpose which I am about to enumerate. They show us the person from the triple standpoints of the *natural*, the *ascetic*, and the *mystic*. When it is a question of a canonized saint, this inquiry has already been made by the Church.

8. — 1° What are this person's **natural qualities**, or what, on the other hand, are his natural defects, whether *physical*, *intellectual*, and, above all, *moral?*

Among those who have known him at different times in his life, has he been regarded as sincere, cool-headed, and of sound judgment, being guided by reason and not by impressions? Briefly, is his mental equilibrium sound? Or, on the contrary, are his descriptions of fact exaggerated, or are they even fabrications? Is his mind weakened by ill health, vigils, fasts, etc.?

If the results are favorable, they prove, with a certain amount of probability, that the chief causes of error enumerated in the last chapter are not to be feared. For such a person's habitual tendencies are calculated to save him from these dangers; but an accidental lapse is possible.

9. — 2° There is an inquiry that relates to the intellectual qualities. It is well to know the **degree of education** that the person has received, what books he has read, and what information he may have acquired by frequenting the society of learned men.

This will sometimes show us that certain revelations are less marvellous than they appear. We were inclined to call them supernatural, because of their erudition or a sublimity for which no other explanation could be found. But we must satisfy ourselves that this knowledge has not been derived from books or the conversation of theologians. We saw this in the case of St. Hildegard further back (Chapter Two, **26**).

10. — *Another application.* In order to prove that **Mary of Agreda's** revelations were divine, she has been described as being, as she herself says, an ignorant girl. But she could read. She was well acquainted with the Bible, which she quotes continually and comments upon. Cardinal Gotti, O.P. (+ 1742), has also shown that several of her revelations were borrowed from an apocryphal (or rewritten) book of the fifteenth century, the *Raptures* of **Blessed Amadeus**,[2] and another, the treatise *On the Nativity of the Blessed Virgin*, falsely attributed to St. Jerome.

Her biographer tells us "that having collected *various treatises* on this devotion [to Mary], she one night conceived a vehement desire to compose one herself" (ch. xix). She confesses to the assistance of theologians. "I have recourse to my director and to my spiritual father in the most delicate and difficult matters" (Part I, No.

Humility leads to their concealment, except in the somewhat rare cases of real utility.

17. — 4° What extraordinary graces of **union** with God does the person believe himself to have received previously, and what has been the verdict regarding them?

If he has merely had strong sentiments of love of God, or even the prayer of quiet, it is best to reserve judgment regarding the revelations and visions, especially if they are of frequent occurrence. It is only in exceptional cases that these graces are granted, unless the soul is much further advanced in prayer.[6]

If, on the contrary, the person has reached the period of ecstasy, there is a probability in favor of the revelation, but nothing more, since the ecstatic saints have sometimes suffered from illusions, and their imagination came into action either during or after the divine visitation.

18. — 5° And, moreover, what **revelations** or visions has he previously believed himself to have received, and what was thought about them? Has he made **predictions**? Were they quite clearly expressed and clearly fulfilled, without its being necessary to resort to subtleties of interpretation?

19. — When an isolated *prediction has come true*, there is sometimes only a probability of its being divine, even when it is a question of human actions that are dependent upon free will. For it may have been uttered at hazard and fulfilled by chance. And then the Devil conjectures many future events, because he knows the habitual trend of both the divine and the human will under similar circumstances. He is especially likely to be correct when it is a question of the populace, who often let themselves be carried away by unreasoning instincts which can be foreseen. Finally, the Devil, after announcing some unwelcome event, can assist in its realization (see St. John of the Cross, *Ascent of Mount Carmel*, Book II, ch. xxi).

20. — We have an instance of a prophecy true in part, but which by its **false elements** had disastrous consequences at the close

of the Great Western Schism. Benedict XIII, the last of the Avignon Popes, escaped to Spain by sea.[7] P. Nider, O.P., relates how, in a town on the seacoast, the Abbot of a monastery warned the inhabitants to be ready to receive the Pope. They laughed at such an unlikely prediction. But the wind, changing suddenly, carried the Pope's ship six miles back upon its course, and obliged it to enter the port in question. Benedict asked the Abbot how he had known of his arrival beforehand. He replied that he had read this prophecy recently in a book, which further said that the same Pope would triumph over all opposition, would return to Rome, and would rule there in peace as before. Seeing that the first part of the prediction was fulfilled, Benedict believed in it, rejected the citation sent by the Council of Constance, was deposed and excommunicated, and died in exile in the Island of Peñiscola (1422) (quoted by Amort, Part II, preface).

21. — Let us now suppose that the predictions made are not fulfilled, and that there is no serious reason for supposing them to be conditional; it is then to be believed that they are not of divine origin.

False prophets do not allow themselves to be easily discouraged by their repeated failures. They always find some good reason to explain them away, or they pretend that the event is only delayed! When necessary, they proceed to confirm their first utterance by some new revelation.

22. — 6° Has this person suffered great **trials** before or after the revelations: sicknesses, contradictions, want of success, or delay in certain enterprises that he had at heart, etc.?

The saints' lives are full of these trials. It is scarcely possible that crosses should not accompany extraordinary graces. For both alike are a mark of God's friendship, and each is a preparation for the other. If, then, a person who was supposed to be in the way of revelations had no crosses, the way would be open to suspicion.

23. — There is one trial in particular that necessarily, as it

were, accompanies these extraordinary ways. Those who know the secrets of these paths, and more certainly still the public, will be inclined to show themselves **skeptical** or **hostile** when they hear them spoken of. "Why, they will say, do these things happen to this person rather than to others who are of greater virtue? It is all due to his imagination! We have no wish to be troubled with these difficult and perhaps unanswerable questions." These criticisms and doubts are an excellent touchstone by which to test the person's humility, patience, and trust in God. If a novice in these virtues, he will meet opposition with words of irritation or discouragement; but if otherwise, he will not be astonished at the divine tarryings, and will continue, in perfect peace, to hope that God's designs will sooner or later be accomplished.

24. — We have a fine **example of** this **patience** in Blessed Juliana, a Cistercian prioress of Mont Cornillon, near Liège (1192-1258). She was chosen by God to institute in the Church the Feast of the Blessed Sacrament. She can be said to have passed her whole life awaiting God's appointed time without ever seeing the realiza-tion of her hopes. Her visions on the subject began two years after her entry into the novitiate. She was then only sixteen (1208). Not until twenty-two years later (towards 1230) does she venture to sub-mit her project to a group of learned theologians. They approved it; but her enemies avenged themselves for her reforms by bringing about the pillaging of her Convent by the populace. Sixteen years later (1246) success seems at last about to arrive; for the Bishop of Liège institutes the Feast in his Diocese. But he dies the same year, and one church alone, the collegiate Church of St. Martin, pays any heed to his order. The Convent is again pillaged. Blessed Juliana, being calumniated, is forced to leave it. She wanders from place to place during the last twenty years of her life, and dies at the age of sixty-six, after a fruitless wait of fifty years' duration. All seemed lost; but an aged Archdeacon of Liège, who had formerly been one of the group of theologians mentioned above, became Pope under the title of Urban IV. Six years after Blessed Juliana's death, in the

Bull of 1264, he instituted the Feast of Corpus Christi for all Christendom, and caused St. Thomas Aquinas to compose the proper Office. But all was not yet completed, for the wars that disturbed Italy caused this Bull to be long forgotten. Finally, in 1316, John XXII celebrated the feast with all solemnity. More than a century had elapsed since the beginning of the revelations! (See *Vie*, by Le Pas; Desclée, 1893).

24 *bis.* — St. Louis Grignon de Montfort, the celebrated missionary in Brittany and La Vendée in the eighteenth century, also showed an heroic trust in God. He had known for some time that he was destined to form two new congregations: that of the *Filles de la Sagesse* (the Daughters of Wisdom), for hospitals and the instruction of poor children, and that of the *Compagnie de Marie* (the Society of Mary [today officially known as the Montfort Missionaries]), composed of missionaries. It was only a year before his death that he was able to inaugurate these two foundations, and he only succeeded in getting together four Sisters on the one hand, and two priests, with a few lay brothers, on the other. The work appeared therefore to be a failure. But St. Louis Grignon knew that the tree would grow. And, in fact, at the beginning of the twentieth century the Daughters of Wisdom numbered 5000, with 44 houses.

25. — The holy souls to whom God commits a mission of utility to the Church are not all thus obliged to submit to the long **martyrdom of hope deferred**. But they have other trials.

As an example of rapid success, we may quote the case of Saint Catherine Labouré, of the Sisters of Charity. She saw in 1832 the striking of the *Miraculous Medal* that had been the subject of her visions only two years before (November, 1830); and she took part in its distribution for forty-four years (1876) without, however, being known to the world.

It was the same with Sister Apolline Andriveau, also a Sister of Charity. In 1846 she received the revelation of the Scapular of the Passion. In the following year Pius IX instituted this devotion. The Sister did not die until forty-seven years later (1894).

26. — 7° Has the person taken **three precautions** that are regarded as indispensable for the avoidance of illusions: (*a*) fearing to be deceived; (*b*) perfect frankness with directors; and (*c*) abstaining from desiring these revelations?

27. — (*a*) It is clear, first of all, that to believe oneself to be **safe from illusions** is an excellent disposition for suffering from them. The soul is then like a city that takes no precautions against the enemy by which it is invested.

Mary of Agreda does not seem to have been penetrated with this fear. On the contrary, she expected that not even her least revelations should be questioned. She declared that God said to her: "I desire that these revelations should be regarded not as opinions, or simple visions, but as *certain truths*" (Part I, No. 10). The Blessed Virgin is quoted as speaking in the same sense: "There is *nothing of yours* in this history, and you can no more attribute it to yourself than *to the pen with which you write it.* You are but the instrument in the Lord's hand.... If anyone fails to believe in what you have written, he will not injure you; *the outrage* will be to me and to my words" (Part III, No. 621; in the French translation, No. 619; and *Lettre à ses religieuses*, No. 9). Thus Sister Mary considers herself securely protected from all error, and that it is a sin not to share her conviction!

28. — (*b*) **Manifestation of the conscience** is necessary. In such difficult matters we must not be both judge and one of the parties concerned. The Devil dissuades us from this sincerity, for, says St. Ignatius, he is afraid to see his wiles unmasked (*Rules for Discernment of Spirits*, First Week, 13), and he abhors such an act of humility.

In revenge he leads us to unbosom ourselves without any reflection to friends who have no authority over us, which enables us to put their advice aside, if it does not please us.

On the other hand, humble souls avoid publicity as much as possible.

29. — (*c*) **The desire for revelations** also exposes the soul to deception. It causes us to find a thousand subtleties by which to substantiate the visions that we believe ourselves to have had, and it excites the imagination to invent new ones.

St. Augustine relates that his mother, **St. Monica**, only just escaped falling into illusion by this means. As she was striving to convert him and bring about his marriage, she wished to know by revelation the outcome of her endeavors. False visions were the result. Happily she had previously enjoyed true visions; she perceived that these differed from the others, "by I know not what kind of relish which she knew not how to express," and she was able to reject these misleading apparitions (*Confessions*, Book VI, ch. xiii).

30. — It therefore follows that a revelation should generally be regarded as doubtful if it has been desired. I say: generally; for in exceptional cases it may happen that this desire has been inspired by the Holy Spirit and is clearly recognized as being from Him.

31. — **Mary of Agreda's** desire to know by revelation the events that she describes is regarded as an unfavorable sign. "This is so sometimes," says Cardinal Gotti, "even in questions of pure curiosity, which in no way help to perfection" (2nd *Censure*, presented to Clement XII; quoted by Mgr. Chaillot). Further examples occur in *La Cité mystique*, Part I, Nos. 4, 33, 52 (where she is occupied with a scholastic question: the order of the divine decrees), 73, 242, 353 (where she wishes to know if in her infancy Our Lady was hungry, how she asked for food, if she wore swaddling clothes, if she cried, if she was treated like a great public figure!); Part II, Nos. 298, 647.

Far from reproving her, her confessors sometimes ordered her to make these indiscreet requests: Part II, Nos. 138 (they wish to know if the Roman Martyrology is correct); 477 (to obtain certain details regarding Our Blessed Lord's birth); 211 (to find the site of St. Elizabeth's house).

3. Nine points upon which information should be obtained, either with regard to the revelation, considered in itself, or the circumstances that accompanied it.

32. — 1° Is there an absolutely **authentic** text? Have not certain expressions been *corrected* as inexact or obscure, or have not certain other passages been actually *suppressed?* These things would be allowable if the edification of the public were the only object. But it is otherwise from the critic's point of view; it means that we are depriving ourselves of very important data.

Instead of curtailments, have there, on the contrary, been *additions* to the revelation? for the sake of accrediting certain doctrines, for instance? This would be a real falsification.

33. — 2° Is the revelation in full accord with the **dogmas and teachings** of the Church, and also with the undoubted pronouncements of history and science?

With regard to dogma, if one sure point alone be contradicted, as has happened many times in supernatural communications, it is sufficient to allow us to affirm that the speaker is not one of God's envoys.

If, on the contrary, a revelation contains no error, a conclusion cannot yet be drawn from this fact alone. The human mind may confine itself prudently within the limits of received truths. The Devil can restrain himself for a time, can give himself the appearance of truth as of holiness, so as to inspire confidence. He resembles those gamblers who intend to cheat; they begin by making their opponents win, that they may afterwards make them lose ten times as much again. It does not hurt him to make some concessions to truth for the sake of insinuating an error. Thus, in communications from spirits you sometimes find pages that are quite correct and (although more rarely) of a high tone of thought; but a dogma will be denied in them. If this snare is successful, the Devil will go further and will teach other errors.

34. — 3° Does the revelation contain no teaching, or is it accompanied by no action that is contrary to decency and **morals**?

In all divine visions there is a perfect propriety of bearing, gestures, and words (Chapter One, **38**).

The aberrations at which certain badly balanced persons have arrived through ignorance of this rule, and their absurd way of understanding what familiarity with Our Lord means, are hardly believable.

If, for example, as has sometimes happened, an apparition professing to be Jesus Christ were to appear without clothing, we might be sure that it was not divine. On this subject see St. Bonaventure (*De profectu religiosorum*, Book II, ch. lxxvi, *alias* lxxv). More obviously still, the instrumentality of the Devil is plain in the case of words or actions that are a clear offence against chastity. God's commandments bind all men without distinction. He dispenses no one under the pretext of friendship. On the contrary, the object of His visit is to lead us further and further away from the life of the senses.

35. — Certain writers, such as Schram (old edition, No. 549; edition of 1848, No. 559), look with suspicion upon a **supernatural revelation** of other people's **vices** and sins, because of the temptation to a lack of charity and an exhibition of contempt or repugnance for certain persons. But this is a matter that depends upon the circumstances of the individual case.

St. John of the Cross says that this knowledge of vices is to be attributed either to God or to the Devil, according to the case in question. "God sometimes represents to holy souls the necessities of their neighbors, *that they may pray for them or relieve them.*"

This utility is a favorable sign, and it is clearly perceived in the numerous saints who possessed the knowledge of the secrets of hearts. By its means they help in the reformation of souls. St. Joseph of Cupertino, St. Catherine of Siena, St. Mary Magdalen of Pazzi, enjoyed this favor so habitually that persons were often unwilling to encounter them without having first cleansed their consciences (Scaramelli, *Tr. du discern.*, No. 28). St. Bridget saw the damnation of several persons. She drew a lesson from this knowledge for others.

On the other hand, says St. John of the Cross again, "He [the Devil] is wont occasionally to reveal, falsely, but with great distinctness, the sins of others, evil consciences, and corrupt souls, *with a view to detraction*" (*Ascent of Mount Carmel*, Book II, ch. xxvi, p. 183).

36. — This knowledge of other people's sins is also often a mere illusion of the imagination. I have known two cases of women who saw visions and who were thus haunted by the rooted idea of the relaxation of **religious Houses**, or the **clergy**. They delighted in discussing these matters, in order, as they said, to bring about a reform. One at least of them has turned out ill. They had no other evidence by which to prove their facts than their revelations, which were sufficiently explained by the propensity of poor human nature to occupy itself with unbecoming subjects. Owing to a perversion of piety, these delirious imaginations finished by yielding to their natural cravings.

In the middle of the nineteenth century another visionary, Cantianille by name, won the confidence of a pious but imprudent Bishop who issued an official publication of the text of her revelation, which was a horrible picture of the morals of the clergy in his diocese. He was obliged to resign. Satan obtained the result that he sought.

It is true that St. Catherine of Siena in her *Revelations* speaks openly and forcibly of the vices of the clergy. But this was in the troublous days of the Great Schism, when the relaxation of the clergy was a matter of common knowledge.

The Secret of Mélanie of La Salette is thought by certain persons to have been modified by the imagination of the person who had the vision. One of the reasons relied on is that the text contains very harsh and unqualified accusations regarding the morals of the clergy and the religious communities from 1846 to 1865.

History speaks quite differently, and indicates a period of fervor and apostolic zeal. It was the time of Pius IX, of Dom Bosco, the Curé d'Ars, etc., and of the spread of Christian teaching throughout France.

37. — 4° Is the information received **useful** for our eternal salvation? We can be sure that revelations are not divine when their subject is simply the acquisition of ordinary matters that are of no utility to souls. God does not go out of His way merely to satisfy curiosity.

It is with revelations as with miracles: they do not occur without a serious motive. They are the works not only of God's power, but of His wisdom.

38. — We see, then, what is to be thought of those prophetesses who pretend to speak in the name of an angel or of a saint, and who at all hours and to all comers give audiences, during which inquiries are made regarding births, marriages, legal proceedings, diseases, the outcome of political events, etc. In spite of the religious *mise en scène*, they are simply fortune-tellers. Nothing is lacking but the conventional pack of cards or coffee grounds. God does not stoop to run an Inquiry Office.

Their clients (although deeply skeptical in many ways) are inspired with confidence by the fact that they are often fortunate in their predictions, and this without either the Devil's aid or being endowed with specially brilliant perceptions. The fact is that they know their trade. A glance enables them to seize the least indication of what they should say, or how they should correct what they have already said. They can even be successful only by replying yes and no at random. For when you play heads and tails, tails have as many chances as heads. They may be right, on an average, five times out of ten in this game. The idle inquirers forget the five unsuccessful cases; they only remember the others, and so sing the prophet's praises.

39. — In **spiritualist** meetings the spirits are often occupied with mere **trifles**. They condescend to reply to idle questions or to provide a drawing-room game. They push furniture about, cause vibrations in musical instruments, and introduce small objects from outside. The medium will amuse you in this way for a whole evening, just as conjurors will do at a fair. Would spirits who have our eternal welfare at heart consent to lend themselves to such childish things? How far removed is all this from the office attributed by theology to our Guardian Angel!

These puerilities become still more distressing when the spirits pose as being our deceased relations, or great philosophers, for if they endeavor to be serious, it is to dictate an appalling tirade of platitudes. Such are the high thoughts that occupy these beings immersed in the light of eternity!

When these spirits claim to be those who were great *savants* on earth, we find that their intellect has become singularly enfeebled in their new life. They are no longer up-to-date in any subject. It has been proved that spiritualistic communications have not advanced science by a single step. No obscure point of history has been cleared up. No mathematical problem has been solved; no chemical formula or theory of physics has been revealed.

Once only Aksakof and other spiritualists thought that they had found an exception. The spirits seemed to have explained a phenomenon that had resisted all the wisdom of men of science. It was a question of the retrograde movement of the satellites of the planet Uranus. But an astronomer, M. Flammarion, went to the root of this assertion and proved that the spirits' explanation was absolutely false (*Les Forces naturelles inconnues*, ch. iii).

40. — A revelation is equally to be regarded with suspicion when its only object is the solving of some **question** that is in **dispute**, whether theological, historical or astronomic, etc. God leaves these discussions to the human intellect because we do not need them for our sanctification. Let us understand that eternal salvation is the only thing of any importance with God. For all else, says St. John of the Cross, it is "always His will that we should make use of our natural endowments" (*Ascent of Mount Carmel*, Book II, ch. xxii, p. 163).

41. — The revelation is also to be mistrusted if, although good from the spiritual point of view, it is a *truism*, occurring in all ascetic writings. God would not employ such great means for such a small result. It is rather probable that the person is thus unconsciously repeating things, that he has learned from books. Or, again, the Devil is amusing him with trifles until the day when, having allayed his suspicions, he can become bolder.

42. — If the **revelations** or **visions** are very numerous, this circumstance, *taken alone*, does not constitute an unfavorable sign.

In fact, no substantial reason can be brought *a priori* for the contrary opinion. And, further, it would be to condemn a number of saints; they have had revelations in very great abundance. Examples: St. Bridget, St. Gertrude, St. Frances of Rome, St. Catherine of Siena, St. Margaret Mary, Ven. Agnes of Langeac, Ven. Marina de Escobar, St. Ignatius, etc. Many have left us enormous volumes, in which, however, everything that they wrote is not included. The opponents of these revelations have never thought of finding fault with this abundance, and no apologist has supposed that objections would be made on this point.

It is true that a letter of St. Francis de Sales (Migne ed., Vol. V, col. 1448) is quoted, which seems to condemn a nun because she had so many visions. But the context shows that the saint was not considering this circumstance alone; it is also stated that these revelations had no practical utility; they were mere words.

43. — We see here how we can **turn** these numerous visions **to account** *indirectly*. We can generally see clearly whether or no they have served any purpose. In the case of an isolated vision the answer might be doubtful.

If the revelations are long or numerous, and if they contain nothing false, indecent, or futile, we may conclude with probability that they do not emanate from the Devil. For if this were so, he would fail in his object. As Samaniégo remarks (*Prologue* to the *Works* of Mary of Agreda, No. 26), it is not possible that he should always continue hidden.

44. — 5° If we examine all the **detailed circumstances** that accompany the vision, the attitudes, gestures, words, etc., do we find the **dignity**, the **gravity**, in keeping with the Divine Majesty? Or, on the contrary, do we not perceive oddities, a grotesque deportment, convulsions, or a lack of restraint that are unworthy even of people who are merely rational and well brought up?

(*a*) This alone should have sufficed to condemn the extraordinary events that took place towards the middle of the eighteenth century at the Saint-Médard cemetery, at the tomb of the deacon Paris. The so-called inspired discourses were extravagant and accompanied by contortions and convulsions; the blows which these persons caused to be inflicted, and their accompanying insensibility to pain, passed as miracles, but they were simply insensate practices, for they did no one any good. I do not speak of the acts opposed to morality that were subsequently added to these hideous scenes. Many Jansenists, however, saw in these things God's manifestations in favor of their teaching.

(*b*) In spiritualistic communications we often find vulgar modes of speech that would offend us in good society. Great historic personages talk a Billingsgate language [a foul-mouthed, abusive way of speaking named after a fish market in London], and if the audience is in sympathy they soon descend to obscenities.

Certain spiritualists are embarrassed by these facts, but they will not on that account admit the instrumentality of the Devil.[8] They prefer to believe that the souls of the dead carry their vices into the other world, and that the offensive replies are given by the dead, who are still liars, or libertines, triflers, hoaxers, etc.

(*c*) In Protestant countries gatherings, called "revivals," are organized from time to time. Crowds weep over their sins, but with a strange exaggeration, a kind of intoxication. We have here, let us not forget it, an excellent principle: ardent sentiments of the love of God and of repentance. But another element which has nothing divine about it, a neurotic exaltation which is contagious, mingles with it. Sometimes imitations of foreign languages, consisting really in a succession of sounds which of themselves have no meaning, are spoken.

45. — When the angels or the saints assume an apparent body in order to manifest themselves, this body never exhibits **deformed limbs** or an animal aspect. It would be unworthy of them. Forms of animals are only met with in very different cases, in symbolic visions, such as Ezekiel's, or St. John the Evangelist's four living creatures [Ezekiel 1:5-14; Revelation 4:6-8]. Perfectly rational allegorical explanations have been given of these forms.

On the other hand, when the Devil appears to those who invoke him, he delights in taking repulsive shapes; he blends the human form with those of the vilest animals. Suarez regards it as being proved "by the admissions of sorcerers themselves," that Satan never reveals himself to them in a completely human shape; there is always a suggestion of something monstrous, such as the feet (*De angelis*, Book IV, ch. xxxv, No. 5).

This idea of Suarez has sometimes been made light of, it being said that he included in this proposition all apparitions of the Devil, not excepting those which Satan wished to pass off as divine. But Suarez does not say a word implying this doctrine; and, indeed, it is not in accordance with the facts.

As de la Reguera (*Theol. myst.*, Vol. II, p. 666, No. 534) and Schram (first edition, No. 507; or No. 517 in the edition of 1848) remark, if the deformity of the apparition were visible, the ruse would be immediately apparent, and the Devil would exhibit a childish want of skill; if it were invisible, hidden either by garments or clouds, the Devil would be ill advised to give himself so much useless trouble making limbs which would not be seen; and, besides, what actual proof would there be of his doing so?

46. — Many authors have repeated, without discussing it, a statement of two seventeenth-century writers (F.F. Thyroeus, 1600, and Del Rio, 1600). According to them, the Devil is never permitted to take the form of a **dove** or of a **lamb** in his apparitions, because these are symbols of the Holy Spirit and of Christ (Schram, *ibid.*).

But this twofold assertion is contradicted by facts, as we see in the life of St. Frances of Rome. For six devils presented themselves to her one day under the form of six beautiful doves. The saint saw through the deception, and they then changed into crows and tried to injure her[9] (Bolland., March 9; First *Life*, Book III, No. 37).

So much for the doves. But there were lambs also. One day the Devil took the form of a lamb that came and lay gently down at the saint's feet. She recognized him, and he became a furious wolf (*ibid.*, No. 23). Another time seven devils appeared to her as white lambs of an engaging appearance, declaring that they symbolized the seven gifts of the Holy Spirit. She again recognized them, and they changed into wolves and tried to attack her (*ibid.*, No. 33).

Another example: The celebrated Magdalen of the Cross, who worked wonders by the Devil's power (Chapter Two, **36**), had an apparition of the Devil one day publicly, under the form of a dove. She claimed that it was the Holy Spirit (Görres, Book VII, ch. xi).

Finally, if the Devil were forbidden to simulate these symbols, he would *a fortiori* be forbidden to represent Christ Himself, which he has sometimes, however, done. If he does not make use of these figures, or does so but rarely, we may attribute it to a much simpler reason: when he tries to entangle us in an illusion he must adopt means that are really powerful, such as the representation of a saint. The person seeing it will at once feel drawn to him by an impulse of devotion. But the sight of a symbolic animal, on the contrary, produces an impression of expectation; it allows time to reflect and to ask ourselves what fruit we can derive from this vision.

In resorting but seldom to these symbols, Satan shows his practical sense. That is all.

If he risked using these unsatisfactory methods with St. Frances, it was for a special reason. The saint often saw symbolic doves or lambs in her visions. There was reason to hope that she would rely on the likeness and accept it from force of habit.

Hitherto it has been a question of *apparitions* of the Devil, wishing to produce an illusion. But there is another very different case, which people forget to distinguish from the preceding: that of the Devil *speaking* during exorcisms. He then sometimes takes the name of an animal symbolizing a vice (see ch. xxiv, **63** [of *The Graces of Interior Prayer*]). Now, he has often stated that God does not permit him to apply to this vile purpose a symbol employed by the Church for holy things. He has declared that he cannot take the name of a dove, a lamb, or of a fish (the symbol of Christ in the Catacombs, because of the Greek word *ichthys*).

47. — Scaramelli seems overly severe in the following case. A person who was by way of seeing frequent visions of the Infant Jesus believed that he had one on Good Friday during a sermon on the Passion. This writer considers it unseemly that on such a day and at such a moment we should fix our thoughts on Our Lord's Infancy. He concludes it to be an illusion (*Traité du discern.*, No. 87).

But this line of reasoning proves too much. It amounts to the general admission that if on some Feast Day, and during a sermon, a spiritual consolation of a different kind takes possession of our souls, we should repulse it. No; there is no sort of obligation to do this. On the contrary, the thought of one mystery of Our Lord's life can throw light upon the others. This author adds that "other reasons had since been found to prove that this person's visions were false." That may be so, but the foregoing reason was worthless.

48. — 6° What **sentiments of peace**, or, on the other hand, **of disquiet**, has the person experienced during the revelation, or subsequently?

St. Ignatius, like St. Catherine of Siena (*Dialogues*, ch. lxxi, English, p. 223), attaches great importance to this means of discernment.

When it is a question of passing inspirations, it may happen that these sentiments are hardly perceptible; but it can scarcely be so in the case of such an extraordinary action as a revelation or a vision, unless, however, it proceeds, not from another spirit, but from our own activity.

49. — This is the **rule** that can be laid down: *With those who are in good faith* (we need speak of no others) **the action of the good spirit** (God or one of His angels) *is characterized by the gift of peace, joy, assurance, and courage, save perhaps at the first moment.*

Let us note this last restriction. At the first moment not only astonishment may be felt, but also anxiety, disquietude, and even fear. But a fuller survey restores the peace of mind. It was thus that the Blessed Virgin was momentarily troubled by the Angel Gabriel's salutation (Luke 1:29). But her calm returned directly, and Mary listened to the message. Holy Scripture refers to the agitation that Abraham experienced, although transiently, in one of his visions (Genesis 15:12); to that of Zechariah, when the Angel Gabriel announced to him that he would be the father of St. John the Baptist (Luke 1:12); of the shepherds at Bethlehem when the angels announced Our Savior's birth (Luke 2:10); of the holy women, at the tomb where the angel was keeping guard (Mark 16:6, 8); of the apostles when the risen Lord appeared among them, and calmed their fears by these words: "Peace be to you" (John 20:19, 26).

The first agitation may also be due to the fact that sensuality or pride rebel against the sacrifice demanded of them. But only the inferior portion of the soul is thus affected.

When he thus gives peace, the good spirit does not act only upon the will, by inclining it gently to good, but upon the intelligence also: the idea seems natural to us, wise, and in conformity with what God would expect of us. Whether as light or as an impulse, God takes possession of the soul without any shock. St. Ignatius explains this way of acting by saying that "the good angel comes with sweetness, peace, suavity, like a drop of water falling on a sponge" (*Rules for the discernment of spirits*, II, 7).

50. — **The Devil's action** has diametrically opposite effects: *when he acts upon those who are of goodwill, he produces, except it may* *be at the first instant, uneasiness, sadness, discouragement, agitation, and darkness.* St. Teresa adds that we often experience these feelings without discovering their cause (*Life*, see especially ch. xxv).

At the first moment there may be a feeling of joy; if we search into the real cause we shall see that the Devil is suggesting some ideas that appeal to our passions or to some earthly tendencies, the desire for honors or sensible pleasures. But in the end his light, like the light of a storm, is scanty, shifting, interspersed with darkness. His activity is enervating, often contradictory, ending in disgust and discouragement. This action, says St. Ignatius, is "like rain in a storm, beating on a rock" (*ibid.*). In short, Satan's inspiration encounters a mysterious resistance in souls of goodwill.

St. Teresa, like St. John of the Cross, often describes the character of the infernal action.[10] The saint explains it thus: "I am thinking whether this may not be so because one spirit is conscious of the presence of another" (*Life*, ch. xxv, 13).

51. — From what has been said, it would seem that when one of these sentiments is well marked, the inference to be deduced from the resulting peace or disquiet affords a sure means of discerning true revelations from the false; because each of the two contrary spirits acts steadily in a contrary way.

When these conditions as to clearness are fulfilled, there would be a moral certainty if we had to decide only between the good spirit and the diabolic spirit. But there is a third action, that of **the human mind.** For example, it will frequently happen that the revelation comes while we are in a state of deep recollection. This state of union will exhibit the character of the divine influence, namely, peace, which may quite well not be disturbed by the natural activity of our own mind even if it comes to the point of simulating supernatural words. It is not from this source that the feeling of peace proceeds, and consequently the peace is not *of itself* sufficient to prove that these words are divine. It only gives a probability to this effect.[11]

And, further, in practice it may be feared lest the person should be under a delusion with regard to the strength and persistence of the sentiment of tranquil joy that has been experienced, for: 1° Has the examination of his interior state been sufficiently exact and complete? 2° Was there not a secret desire to obtain such a counsel, such a reply from God? What he felt would then be a purely natural joy at seeing his ideas approved.

52. — Desiring to punish a presumptuous feeling in **St. Catherine of Bologna** (Poor Clare) at the outset of her religious life, God permitted that she should not detect the diabolic action for some length of time, in spite of the disquiet that accompanied it. Feeling herself favored with great graces, she had said audaciously to the Devil: "Know that you could send me no temptation without my perceiving it?" After this imprudent challenge she had false apparitions of Our Lord and the Blessed Virgin for five years. They reproached her with a lack of abnegation and obedience to her Superior; but she could not find out what it was that they required of her; then, as she afterwards endured violent temptations against these two virtues, she took the temptations for sins. All this threw her into a state of anguish. At the same time she fell into a dreadful aridity. What saved her from despair was the opening of her conscience to her Superior. God finally enlightened her completely with regard to this temptation (Bolland., March 9, Second *Life*, No. 10 and following).

53. — 7° It often happens that a revelation leads to the execution of some bold **enterprise**; the establishing of a new devotion, for instance, the foundation of a religious Congregation or pious Association, the remodelling of the constitutions of another, the correction of the relaxed state of a certain group of persons, the building of a Church, the inauguration of some work for which the available resources are insufficient, the preaching of a more refined spirituality which God is supposed to have reserved for our time (as being less gross, they say, than those that went before, etc.).

In this case it is necessary to see if the work is: (*a*) *good in itself* and in conformity with the spirit of the Church; (*b*) *useful,* and of a utility that explains such an exceptional means as a revelation; (*c*) *opportune*, if it truly responds to a new need; (*d*) if it injures any similar work which it would be better to support. (For the rest of the practical conduct of the matter, see Chapter Four.)

54. — Amort says that the revelations of women are probably false when they lead to a wish to direct **clergy and princes** and to teach them, speaking with an air of authority. For this is not the part that women should play in the Church — at least, not as a regular practice (*Sommaire des Règles*, 3, rule 30). He instances this prudent trait in the Ven. Louis du Pont. He was director to the Ven. Marina de Escobar, and approved of her revelations as a whole, and was afterwards their editor. But he would never believe in those that she often thought she received from her Guardian Angel, indicating various counsels that she was to transmit to the King regarding the management of his Court (Part I, ch. viii, Rule 24).

55. — **Mary of Agreda**, on the contrary, kept up a correspondence with Philip IV of Spain for twenty years. The King divided each sheet of his letters into two columns, and wrote upon the first only. The Sister replied upon the other. M. Germond de Lavigne has published a French translation of forty of these double letters. They are quite commonplace, and consist in general advice that anyone could have given. It is strange, too, that this Sister, who was so in the habit of receiving revelations, had none regarding the King's relaxed morality and his culpable carelessness concerning affairs for which he was responsible. And yet she was in a position to exercise a great influence over her correspondent. Many of the letters amount to nothing more than the vague declaration that she is interested in the preoccupations made known to her by the King; 614 other letters have been published in Spain.

56. — 8° Have the revelations stood the test of **time** and **scrutiny?**

Without this condition, the favorable judgments that may have been passed upon them are not a sufficient guarantee. Amort thinks that it is only in exceptional cases that a revelation can be regarded as assured until after the death of the person who received it (Part I, ch. iv).

In any case, when the revelations form a *series*, having a fixed object, such as the inauguration of a pilgrimage, we must allow events to unfold themselves and wait to pronounce an opinion until the vision has announced that the series has come to an end.

If during this long period of waiting the revelation withstands all attacks, there is a great probability of its truth.

57. — 9° If the object of the revelation was to institute a new devotion, have subsequent events clearly shown that God favored this work in a special manner? For example, has it produced **great fruits** of grace on all sides? Have the Sovereign Pontiffs, the Bishops, favored its progress? This character is found in a marked degree in the Scapular of Mount Carmel, the devotion to the Sacred Heart and the Miraculous Medal.

---

4. *Conclusions to be drawn from the preceding data*

58. — In enumerating the points upon which it is necessary to inform ourselves, we have seen that a certain number of characters belong peculiarly to true revelations and visions, and others to those that are false.

When we have to prove that the action comes from the Devil, one of these signs alone is so clear at times that there is no room for doubt. But this is not so when it is a case of proving that the action is from God with no admixture of another action; we have seen that *no one character*, **taken alone**, then *leads to certainty*.

Is the problem insoluble, then, when there is no miracle to confirm the revelation? Must we always resign ourselves to possessing a slight probability only? In a word, will the conditions that are regarded as necessary never be sufficient? Here is the reply.

59. — Principle. *Given that we desire to judge of the truth of one or more revelations, at least when taken as a whole, we may regard it as very probable, sometimes even as morally certain, that the conditions are SUFFICIENT, if those that are commonly regarded as NECESSARY are all verified, and in an unmistakable way.* — The assurance is so much the stronger as the characters are more striking.

60. — In order to prove this proposition, we can begin by bringing an **argument based on authority**. Gerson, who has made a special study of these questions, formulates the principle under an equivalent form.

"We may," he says, "be mistaken if we consult one sign only or a few; we must group a number of them together (*plura in unum conglobentur*)" (*De probatione spirituum*, Consid. 6). Schram adds: "The more numerous these favorable signs, the greater will our assurance be. From this assemblage (*ex horum signorum collatione*) we shall with prudence deduce, according to the particular case, a more or less strict *certainty* or a strong or medium or weak *probability*, or a favorable *conjecture*, or, on the contrary, an uncertainty which will cause us to suspend our judgment" (Old edition, No. 572; 1848 edition, No. 582).

Amort (Part I, ch. vi, Rule 22) adopts a like attitude.

It may be said that, although the above principle has not been laid down by the majority of writers, the universal practice in all times and in all places has implicitly taken it for granted. We find that all authors, having to discuss the value of a revelation, content themselves with reviewing characters that, taken alone, are not a sufficient proof that the revelation is divine. If, however, the signs are favorable, they consider themselves justified in concluding it to be so, without any other explanation. They therefore admit by implication that these necessary characters are sufficient when they are found together.

61. — Arguments based on reason. 1° No other principle except this one has ever been formulated in order to establish the fact that a revelation is very probable or morally certain. If we refuse, then, to accept it, we have to say that the Church should have maintained a strictly reserved attitude regarding numberless revelations that have been made to the saints in the last 2000 years. It would have been a mistake to think it possible ever to depart from this expectant attitude.

2° It has always been admitted as a law of Divine Providence that God never permits evil to have *all* the characters of good. What will be the signs that can warn souls of goodwill? We cannot say beforehand, but they will be there. The wisdom and goodness of God require that this should be so. Therefore, if the examination of a revelation has been conscientious, if the man has done all that he could for his enlightenment, and if God has allowed no signs of falsity to appear, we can conclude from this assemblage of circumstances that God wishes us to regard it as probable, and sometimes even as morally certain.

62. — **Objection.** In these researches must one *always* be afraid of having overlooked a circumstance that would have aroused serious doubts?

63. — **Reply.** No; not always, for these problems have been put so often that the conditions "commonly received" practically include all that can be said in the matter.

The same objection could be made in all the problems of the moral order: for instance, You have come to regard such a man as honest, thanks to your long relations with him and the general opinion regarding him. Who knows whether you have observed him sufficiently? Or again: The critics admire the high literary excellence of such and such a work; all the rules seem to be in its favor. But perhaps there is one that has been forgotten, and which would be sufficient to change the verdict? And yet in these questions everyone allows that we can *sometimes* arrive at a certainty.

64. — The real **drawback** to the above method is that it requires much time and labor. But we must resign ourselves to this. It would certainly be much more convenient to have to verify two

or three obvious characteristics only, furnishing evidence beyond dispute. In the same way, in deciding whether a book is a master-piece, one would like to be able to settle the matter by putting a few short questions; and so also when forming an opinion concern-ing a man's honesty. But this ideal cannot be realized in things that relate to the moral order.

65. — According to the above pronouncement, a revelation may possess divine characteristics as a whole without this being so with regard to all the details. In fact, the reasons that prove the worth of the complete revelation are not always sufficient to justify all the elements of which it is composed.

66. — Short of positive proof to the contrary, however, the details have the benefit of the verdict pronounced upon the whole. The presumption is in their favor.

67. — In order to judge whether **ecstasies** are divine, we shall act upon the same principles as in the case of revelations, after hav-ing inquired into the person's character.

The two chief points of evidence are as follows: 1° How has the soul been occupied while thus deprived of the use of the sen-sible faculties? Was it taken captive by intellectual knowledge of the higher order, carried away by an immense love? 2° What was the degree of virtue before attaining to this state, and what great progress has resulted from it afterwards?

If the replies are favorable, the probabilities are on the side of the divine ecstasy. Neither the Devil nor disease can carry imita-tion to this point.

As to the physiological effects, no conclusions can be drawn from them, as a rule. The alienation of the sensible faculties can quite well present the same appearances in a divine ecstasy and in its counterfeits.

There may, however, be added certain phenomena that dis-pose of the hypothesis of disease and reveal a supernatural cause, whether divine or no: levitation, for example.[12]

68. — With certain persons, in very close union with God, the slow study of the various signs has sometimes been aided, or even replaced, by a **supernatural intuition.** This is what is called the infused gift of the discernment of spirits; the other is termed *acquired.*

Scaramelli defines this infused gift as "an instinct or a light given by the Holy Spirit to discern correctly, in oneself or in others, the principle from which the soul's interior movements proceed; whether it is good or bad" (*Discern.*, No. 21).

69. — In some pious persons' lives we find that they have not only asked God in a general way to **confirm** such and such a project or revelation **by a sign**; but they themselves fixed the sign, and especially its value as a mark of certainty saying: If such an event takes place, I shall regard it as indicating that God desires such and such a thing. Can we rely on this sign?

We will leave out of the question the exceptional cases where the request is prompted by an inspiration of the Holy Spirit. By this fact in itself we possess the certainty that God will reply by means of the event.

Let us suppose the contrary case. If a true and personal miracle has been asked for and it has taken place, God thus gives His approval.[13] But more often He will not hear our request, it being an indiscretion to make it. This was why the Curé of Lourdes did not obtain the sign that he desired. He said to Bernadette: "Ask the Lady, in proof of the holiness of her apparitions, that the wild mountain rose, now all shrivelled from the winter cold, shall blossom in this month of February." The wild rose did not blossom, but God worked a much more useful miracle: a spring gushed forth.

Blessed Angela of Foligno asked Our Lord, as a proof of the divine nature of His apparitions, to give her a precious stone or to light the taper that she had in her hand. Our Lord refused to give her this miraculous sign: "That which you ask for is a sign which would give you joy only when you touch it, but it would not draw you out of doubt, and in such a sign you might well be deceived.

But I will give you another sign, better than the one you have asked for; and this sign shall be continually with you, inwardly in your soul, and you shall always feel it. Moreover, this shall be the sign: you shall ever be fervent in love, and in the love of God, and en-lightened by the knowledge of God within you. And let this be a most certain sign to you, that it is I, because no one can make this sign, save I alone. And this is the sign that I place inwardly in your soul, and that is better than the other that you requested: I place in you a love of Me, by which your soul will become inebriated, and fervent, and constantly glowing by reason of Me, so that you will desire to suffer tribulations for the love of Me. And if anyone shall say or do you evil, you will take it as a favor, and will cry out that you are unworthy of such a grace" (*Visions and Instructions of Blessed Angela of Foligno*, ch. xxix, pp. 104-105).

70. — We will now suppose that the event asked as a sign is **not miraculous**. If it takes place, the circumstances accompanying it can, with all probability, show the will of God, provided that all human means of information have previously been resorted to.

This last precaution appears in the life of the Rev. Mother Marie de la Providence. Before taking an important decision she frequently fixed upon a sign and was heard on account of her im-mense confidence in the divine goodness. But she acted thus after much prayer and having realized the expediency of the decision. The fresh sign that she sought was only the final confirmation of several others, showing that it was time to act. Sometimes this sign was the sudden arrival of the sum of money or other aid that was necessary for the enterprise, and then it was more than a sign — it was also the means of realizing the project. If the event asked for does not take place, or if, on the contrary, it occurs without having been preceded by the precautions already indicated, we can draw no conclusions. God will often allow the operation of secondary causes, while He stands, as it were, apart. You have had the temer-ity to impose conditions upon Him without observing the requi-site forms; you have limited Him to the summary alternative of a throw of the dice, which you consider is the equivalent of a revelation. He may refrain from intervening.

St. Ignatius, at the beginning of his conversion, exposed himself in this way to making a deplorable choice in a serious matter. He was travelling with a Muslim who blasphemed against the Blessed Virgin. The saint, who was still full of the maxims of Chivalry, asked himself if he ought not to avenge the honor of the Mother of God with the miscreant's blood. The Devil would naturally encourage St. Ignatius in an illusion which would have resulted in his conviction for homicide. Finally, he decided that, according as his horse should turn to the right or the left at the next crossways, he would attack his enemy or not. God was not obliged to fall in with this contrivance; but as He had designs with regard to St. Ignatius, He protected him. The horse turned to the left, although there were obstacles in the way. Later on, when he was better instructed in the spiritual life, he pointed out less expeditious but surer methods of discovering God's will.

70 *bis.* — **The gift of tears.** I have spoken elsewhere of tears shed during ecstasy (ch. xiii, **10** [of *The Graces of Interior Prayer*]). Let us now treat a more general question. It is said that a person has the gift of tears when certain pious thoughts cause him to weep often and abundantly, and when this facility can only be attributed to the divine action. This has been the case with many saints.

The restriction that concludes the definition is an important one. Tears may, in fact, come from other causes than the divine action. The Devil can produce them, either to enfeeble the health or to give rise to pride (see **71**, 3°). Much more frequently they may be the result either of an oversensitive nature, which often happens with women, or persons of a neurotic condition. In the present stage of knowledge it is difficult to define the exact part played by the temperament.

70 *ter.* — **Line of conduct to be followed** by the director. It would be too difficult for him to seek to distinguish clearly between

God's action and that of the Devil. It is sufficient that he should inform himself on two practical points:

1° What is the *immediate origin* of these tears? Are they solely emotions produced by a religious thought: love, joy, sorrow for sins, gratitude, compassion for Our Lord's sufferings, etc.? It is this that gives the value to tears; without this circumstance they would be an unimportant physiological phenomenon.

2° *Are* the tears detrimental to the health?

If the replies to these two questions are favorable, there is a greater or lesser probability that the action is divine; at any rate, there is nothing blamable. The soul, then, will be left in tranquillity, but the individual should be warned to be on guard. In the contrary case, the director will not go so far as to forbid the tears, for their suppression is not directly in the penitent's power. But he will employ indirect means: (*a*) he will try to direct the thoughts to less moving subjects; (*b*) and develop the conviction that the phenomenon, being physical, has no value.

EXTRACTS
*How the Devil sometimes inclines us to certain virtues;
Signs of his action*

---

71. — St. Teresa:

1° "I told you elsewhere how the Devil frequently fills our thoughts with great schemes, so that instead of putting our hands to what work we can do to serve our Lord, we may rest satisfied with working to perform impossibilities" (*Interior Castle*, Seventh Mansion, ch. iv, 21).

2° Another "sign of the Devil's presence" [is that] "the soul is thrown into a state of disgust, and is troubled... for if it conceives good desires, they are not strong; its humility is fictitious, disturbed and without sweetness" (*Life*, ch. xxv, 17). In short, this action weakens and distresses. The divine action, on the contrary, strengthens and brings peace.

3° "Some persons seem as if they could never stop crying: believing that tears are beneficial, they do not try to check them nor to distract their minds from the subject, but encourage them as much as possible. The Devil seizes this opportunity to weaken them so that they become unable to pray or to keep the Rule" (*Interior Castle*, Sixth Mansion, ch. vi, 7).

4° Describing how she at times felt such an extreme horror of her sins as almost led her to despair: "This is but a false humility, and Satan invented it for the purpose of disquieting me and trying whether he could thereby drive my soul to despair.... That it is his work is clear from the restlessness and discomfort with which it begins, and the trouble it causes in the soul while it lasts; from the obscurity and distress, the aridity and *indisposition for prayer and for every good work*, which it produces. It seems to stifle the soul and trammel the body, so *as to make them good for nothing*. Now though the soul acknowledges itself to be miserable, and though it is painful to us to see ourselves as we are, and though we have most deep convictions of our own wickedness... yet true humility is not attended with trouble; it does not disturb the soul" (*Life*, ch. xxx, 10, 11).

72. — St. Ignatius:

"As soon as the Devil sees us to be humble, he strives to inspire us with a false humility, that is to say, an excessive and vicious humility" (First Letter to Sister Rejadella).

Notes

---

[1] A miracle came thus to encourage St. Teresa at the beginning of her reform which she had been commanded to undertake by revelations. While secretly building her future Convent at Avila she arranged that her sister, Juana de Ahumada, and her brother-in-law, Juan de Ovalle, should live there; they thus seemed to be building a

house for themselves, and in this way the opponents of her scheme suspected nothing. Going one day to inspect the works, the saint brought to life again her five-year-old nephew, Gonsalvo, who had been struck down by the fall of a wall and had lain lifeless for several hours (1561). Taking into account the circumstances of time and place, this miracle was the sign of God's approbation of the enterprise and of the idea that had inspired it.

² A Franciscan, confessor to Sixtus IV. Skies of crystal occur here. Sister Mary especially takes from him the idea of Our Lord's Body being formed out of three drops of blood from Our Lady's heart. I will merely point out two physiological errors in such a doctrine. To begin with, it implies the circulation of the blood, the discovery of which was quite recent (1628), to have been still unknown at Agreda. Since all the blood passes through the heart, no special privilege can be attached to it, and there is no further reason for presenting it as a marvellous symbol of Mary's sentiments. And, further, there is an error with regard to the function of the blood. It is as powerless as milk to create tissue or to dispose it after a given plan; it serves to nourish the already existing tissues. God can gain nothing by thus changing the course of nature.

³ M. Flournoy has given the name *cryptomnesia* to this fact, that certain forgotten items of knowledge reappear without being recognized by the subject, who henceforth regards them as something new.

⁴ In the *Lives* of the Saints, in that of the Holy Curé d'Ars, for instance, we read of fasts and vigils which would be indiscreet for many of us. They would reduce our strength and, more serious still, would weaken our faculties. We have even known cases of saints who have gone without food for several weeks. Whence is this different standard of conduct for them and us? It is that God aids them miraculously, and they *are aware* of this fact. They know that they can go to such or such lengths, *physically* and *morally* either because they have received an extraordinary light, or because they have made a series of attempts, as St. Ignatius advises in his *Rules for Temperance* (Rule 4).

⁵ St. Teresa: If "the soul receives favors and caresses from Our Lord, let it examine carefully whether it therefore rates itself more highly; if self-abasement does not increase with God's expressions of love, certainly they do not come from the Holy Spirit" (*Interior Castle*, Sixth Mansion, ch. iii, 2).

⁶ I have been told of two persons who for a long time have been having visions and locutions of Our Lord, and who yet have never, it appears, experienced the mystic union with God or with the Sacred Humanity of Jesus.

⁷ It was probably the first voyage (1408). The Pope went from Italy to Port-Vendres, which, like Roussillon, belonged at that time to Spain.

⁸ Spiritualists lay it down as a principle that spirits holding communication with them are the spirits of the dead only, or, to use their language, disembodied spirits. In order to be sure that such or such a spirit is one of their own relations or friends, they have one proof only — namely, that the spirit in question should acquaint them with a secret known only to themselves and the dead. But the answer is that this reason is not sufficient. For they admit that during our lives we are surrounded by spirits that know all our secrets. One of these may therefore act the part of a dead relative and mystify us.

⁹ Instead of the word *crow*, which is in the Italian text, the Bollandists say *deer*; this is

a printer's error. An "e" has been substituted for an "o," *cervorum* for *corvorum* (this was remarked by Dom Rabory, author of a *Life* of the saint).

[10] Speaking of intellectual visions of Our Lord: "She was conscious of His being at her right hand, although not in the way we know an ordinary person to be beside us, but in a more sublime manner, which I cannot describe.... It brings with it such *graces* and effects as could not come from melancholia nor from the Devil. If they did, the soul would not be so filled with *peace* and a constant desire to please God, with an utter contempt of all that does not lead to Him. Consequently, my friend recognized this to be no work of the evil one, as Our Lord showed her more and more clearly....

"This favor brings with it an overwhelming sense of self-abasement and humility; the reverse would be the case did it come from Satan... I believe it to be impossible for the Devil to produce an illusion lasting so long, nor could he benefit the soul so greatly, nor give rise to *such interior peace*. It is not his way, nor, *if he would, could* such an evil creature bring about so much good.... The mind's continual keeping in the presence of God and the concentration of its thoughts on Him would so enrage the fiend that, though he might try the experiment once, he would not often repeat it" (*Interior Castle*, Sixth Mansion, ch. viii, 4, 5, 9).

[11] Suarez: "This sign gives a strong probability, but does not amount to infallibility" (*De Relig.*, Tr. X, Book IX, ch. x, No. 37).

[12] I do not speak of aureoles. For we may ask ourselves whether they have not a natural foundation. In fact, Dr. C. Feré states that he observed the head and hands of two hysterical patients to become luminous, of an orange color, during their attacks. With the first, the light extended to a distance of seventy centimeters from the head (*Revue de Médecine*, April 10, 1905, Alcan). It is regrettable that no photograph was taken of this phenomenon, which might be disputed on account of its extreme rarity. In such a case we might ask ourselves whether the observations were carried out with all desirable precautions.

In the same way, many saints have emitted agreeable odors during their lifetime or at death. These odors were various; they resembled those of the violet or the rose, orange blossom, cinnamon, musk, benjamin, etc. We can no longer admit that this was a miracle *in itself*, but only in virtue of the circumstances (which should be examined in each concrete case). In fact, doctors have observed, although rarely, a certain number of maladies in which the above-named odors are produced. In diabetic persons, in particular, suffering from acetonemia, we find an odor closely resembling that of a russet apple. In a normal state, the derivatives of alcohol (aldehydes and acetones) resulting from digestion are oxidized; but in certain troubles of the nervous system and of the interior nutrition of the tissues these bodies, perspiration, etc., escape by the breath (see Dr. G. Dumas' article in the *Revue de Paris* of Dec. 1, 1907).

[13] We may regard as almost miraculous the sign that Rev. Mother Marie de la Providence, foundress of the Helpers of the Holy Souls, asked for; but she only made the request in obedience to her director, F. Aussant, O.P. The circumstances seem to prove that he had received a true revelation. The newly formed community was contemplating leaving a cramped and insanitary dwelling-place and buying a house. The Director said: "Since you have such trust in Providence, pray that God will lead you where He wills. Then pass down the Rue de Sèvres, the Rue de Vaugirard, and the Rue du Cherche-Midi; but do not trouble to read the notice boards be-

cause it will be in one of the *cross streets running* into these that you will find the home destined for you. Go straight on, therefore, and when you hear in your heart something that says 'Turn,' you will turn." The Mother carried out the order, and felt the interior movement at the corner of the Rue de la Barouillère. Here she found a house for sale, and heard an interior locution which assured her that this would be the Motherhouse. This did not prevent her making use of human methods, such as visiting and inspecting the house (*Notice* on her Life).

CHAPTER FOUR

RULES OF CONDUCT

1. Seven rules for the director

1. — *First rule.* To resign himself to a **slow progress.** We have seen that much time and labor are required before we can pronounce an opinion concerning the truth of revelations. Instead of pressing forward, the director must know how to rest content with provisional judgments. He will have to be on his guard against his own precipitation and that of his penitent. This latter will be questioning him incessantly, and saying: "Tell me whether these extraordinary things really come from God, or if you attribute a part, at any rate, to the imagination," etc. In such cases we may reply: "These delays are inevitable. While the full light is not granted, to give a definite approval to your visions and projects would be an imprudence. It may be your own fault that the light continues insufficient. It is for you, by your prayers and sacrifices, to obtain that some more certain signs be given to us."

Often, too, the director will be urged on to a premature decision by people who are well-intentioned, but who have no idea of the precautions with which we have to surround ourselves. "What is the use," they will say, "of suspending judgment in this fashion? Take the simplest, and usually the safest way, and declare that God is not the author of these extraordinary occurrences." But we should thus be exposing ourselves to illusions. For, as Scaramelli tells us, quite as many err in taking God's favors for diabolic works as by doing the reverse (*Discern.*, No. 213).

2. — *Second rule.* **Not to display admiration** for these visions, *even if they appear to be real.* On the contrary, he will prove that they are less estimable than the mystic union, and particularly than the practice of the virtues. In this way he will be keeping to the truth, and, at the same time, will have the advantage of being protected from endless and insignificant details.

3. — *Third rule.* To be **gentle** in his treatment of the person. *If the visions appear to him suspicious,* not to show his distrust harshly. He will only intimidate penitents, which would lead to their hiding important details. While admitting his doubts, he can show a kindness that will set them at their ease. It may not be a person's own fault, if he is himself deceived. St. Teresa and St. John of the Cross both advise this gentleness (see Extracts, No. **39**). Let him strive with prudence, however, to enlighten them with regard to these illusions. This is the way to cure them. But they will be confirmed in them if the visions are rejected without any explanation. They will fancy themselves the victim of prejudice. Knowing that true revelations are accompanied by trials, they will falsely persuade themselves that the trials suffice to prove the truth of their revelations.

To sum up, let the director's language be neither harsh nor ironical.

4. — *Fourth rule.* To bear in mind the **end** to which the visions, and especially the revelations, tend. He must exhibit a proportionately stronger **mistrust** if it is a question of a matter having consequences of greater magnitude.

5. — **Three cases** may present themselves:

(*a*) This end may be *solely* to augment the love of God, of Our Lord, the Blessed Virgin, and the saints in the seer of the vision. Such an end is good. Nothing then hinders our regarding these visions or even these revelations *provisionally* as divine, and accepting them after an earnest examination; but we must be on our guard, and satisfy ourselves from time to time that this continues to be the sole end.

Thus we need not interfere with a person who, without being very far advanced in other ways, believes himself often to enjoy the intellectual presence of Our Lord; but without revelations.

(*b*) The object may be to *instruct* the person who sees the vision. More precautions are needed here. Such an instruction should be watched (see 24).

And it is the same if there are predictions. We must have very strong proof of their divine origin to allow of their being communicated to others than the director or Superiors.

(*c*) Finally, the revelation may urge some enterprise.

It is here especially that great caution is necessary. The mere affirmation, even of one who is closely united to God, is never sufficient. We have seen, on the contrary (Chapter Three, 53), how the matter must be examined by the sober light of reason and submitted to *prudent* and *learned* men. In this way, if the advice received by the revelation is followed, and if, later on, this revelation should be recognized as false, there will be no reason for regretting the work that has been undertaken. All that the revelation will have done will be to have *suggested* an idea; it will have been accepted, as would have been the case if it had come from a person endowed neither with authority nor any special guarantees. It is merely the *occasion* of any decisions that are taken.[1]

6. — As a matter of fact, the Church has not proceeded otherwise in instituting certain **Feasts or devotions** which have had their origin in a revelation. The revelation itself continues on the footing of a pious opinion, having nothing obligatory about it. But its results are of service to souls; this is what the Church looks to.

7. — This **reserve on the Church's part** appears in the institution of the Feast of Corpus Christi. Urban IV sets forth the reasons in a special Bull, and it is only at the end that he makes a vague

and very brief allusion to the revelations that had asked for the institution of this Feast (see Chapter Three, 24). They only occur as accessories.

The public cultus rendered to the Sacred Heart was brought about by revelations to St. Margaret Mary. But it contained in itself all that was necessary for approval; so that the revelations merely suggested the idea. They are not even mentioned in the Mass for the Feast.

In 1832 the Miraculous Medal was circulated everywhere, following upon St. Catherine Labouré's visions, but leaving the verdict regarding these visions on one side. It was merely stated that this devotion was good in itself. And it was the same in 1846 with the Scapular of the Passion, due to the revelations made to Sister Andriveau (Chapter Three, 25). Pius IX approved it at once, without insisting upon any official inquiry into its origin.

When in June, 1899, Leo XIII publicly dedicated the whole world to the Sacred Heart, it was after requests had been addressed to him by Mother Mary of the Divine Heart, Superior of the Order of the Good Shepherd at Oporto. But he would not allow his decision to be based on Mother Mary's revelations. Cardinal Mazzella and the Sacred Congregation of Rites relied solely upon the theological reasons.[2]

8. — Sister Andriveau's life furnishes us with an interesting **confirmation** of the motives by which the Church acts. She had presented another proposition that had not been listened to, although she believed it to be founded upon a revelation like the other (Letter of April 25, 1849). But the idea did not appear to be a wise one. According to the Sister, Our Lord wished Pius IX to establish a Feast of the Passion during Easter week. There were serious reasons for seeing an illusion here, for it is in the spirit of the Church to preserve the distinctive characters of penance or of joy to certain seasons of the year. At Easter time we rejoice in the Resurrection; it would have necessitated a sudden return to sentiments of penitence and compassion; and this when we have been devoting our-

selves to them all during Lent and Holy Week. This illusion, more-over, is explained by the special devotion to the Passion that domi-nated Sister Andriveau's life.

9. — This same way of acting on the Church's part shows itself also with regard to certain **pilgrimages** which have for their origin a fact that is regarded as historic; those, for instance, of Lourdes, La Salette, Pontmain, Loreto, or the apparition of St. Michael at Monte Gargano, etc.

In these cases the Pope approves or encourages the pilgrim-age, but without guaranteeing the historic fact by his infallibility. Also belief in it is not obligatory. The fact is regarded as resting upon a human testimony having as great a probability as a host of oth-ers. Criticism can be applied to it. What the Church gives as the object of the devotion of the pilgrimage is the saint himself, who is honored there. This homage and these prayers are not exposed to any illusion.

9 *bis.* — These invariable rules of the Church appear in the question of the pilgrimage to Notre-Dame de **Pellevoisin**, founded in 1876 after a revelation. By a decree of April 4, 1900, the Sacred Congregation of Rites had approved the pictures and statues, but with this noteworthy restriction, that they insisted on an alteration of certain details, which, however, were signified in the vision, and also of the title taken by Our Lady on the occasion. They had acted in the same way with regard to the Scapular and the corresponding Arch-confraternity. Many persons concluded from these approba-tions that Rome recognized the truth of the apparitions whence these devotions proceeded. The diocese of Bourges became the the-ater of violent discussions on this subject, and the Archbishop, who was considered overcautious, was attacked. Then, by a decree of September 8, 1904, the Holy Office informed this prelate that the above-named approbations implied "no approbation, whether di-rect or indirect, of no matter what apparitions, revelations, graces of healing and other similar facts which might be related concern-ing the said Scapular or the said pious confraternity."

10. — Many **religious congregations** have been founded after revelations. But these have been only an accessory, a spur to undertake a work that, considered on its own merits, was judged worthy of performance, and which responded to some fresh need.

11. — **St. Teresa**, under circumstances of grave importance, wished that her advisers should not be influenced in their decision by her revelations. It was a question of an important stroke of policy, of breaking with her old Convent at Avila and founding a rival House in the same town, where the reform would be inaugurated. The saint wished to have the advice of a learned Dominican, Fr. Ybanez. He began by thinking this idea a piece of folly, but soon became its supporter. "She made known to him the motives that had decided her to engage in this enterprise; without speaking, however, of the order that she had received from Our Lord, or of her revelations or other supernatural favors" (*Histoire*, by a Carmelite of Caen, Vol. I, ch. xii).

A modern hagiographer is astonished that in this conjuncture, and for a considerable time, Fr. Balthasar Alvarez, the saint's Confessor, should not have ventured to take any decision either on one side or the other. But besides the fact that his Superior prevented him at that time from compromising himself in a very critical enterprise, he had not made up his mind about all the graces of which his penitent spoke to him. Now that St. Teresa is canonized, it is easy to pronounce against those who thwarted her. But she was then only Sister Teresa. They felt misgivings concerning the extraordinary way in which she was led, and with the more reason that in Spain they were suffering, according to La Fuente's expression, "from an epidemic of pious fanatics, the victims of hallucinations" (*facsimile* of the manuscript of the *Life*, ch. xxiii). What should we do nowadays under similar circumstances?

12. — As a contrast with the prudence displayed by St. Teresa and her directors, let us recall the deplorable facility with which **Mme Guyon** believed in her own revelations and in her divine mission, as she claimed it to be; a facility imitated by Fr. La Combe and Fénelon, who became her directors, or rather her associates and her disciples. The consequences that resulted were disastrous to them.

Fr. La Combe, who had impregnated himself with Molinos' ideas in Rome, could not fail to be filled with Mme Guyon's quietist notions. They both believed themselves to be called to an extraordinary apostolate (1686). "I felt my soul sealed," she says, "for a mission similar to that of the Apostles when they received the Holy Spirit" (*Vie*, by herself, Vol. II, p. 16). For seven years they set themselves to preach quietism on all sides, in Switzerland, at Turin, at Grenoble (where Mme Guyon tried in vain to win over the Carthusians, who, however, consented to hear her), at Verceil, Marseilles, and Paris. Their connection ceased in 1688 when, by the King's orders, Fr. La Combe was confined in the Bastille and underwent a series of trials that drove him out of his mind.

About a year after this separation, Mme Guyon obtained a rapid ascendency over Fénelon's mind.[3] She made his acquaintance at the house of Mme de Béthune, on the outskirts of Versailles. "I was suddenly, with extreme force and sweetness, interested [in] him. It seemed to me Our Lord *united him to me very intimately*, more so than anyone else. My consent was asked for. I gave it. Then it appeared to me that, as it were, a spiritual filiation took place between him and me" (*Autobiography of Mme Guyon*, Vol. II, Part III, p. 218, translated by T.T. Allen).[4]

12 *bis.* — It is surprising to see such an intelligent man as Fénelon allow himself to be so quickly won over and directed by a woman of no culture. Thirty-seven years of age, and director of the fashionable world, he was in no wise led by an earthly passion, for the lady had reached forty and was disfigured by smallpox. But he felt a curiosity, a need to meet a saint who should reveal to him the secrets of Heaven, and he ignored the precautions that should be taken with prophetesses who wish to take possession of an influential person. "He saw her," said Saint-Simon; "their minds were pleasing one to the other and their sublimity mingled. I do not know

whether they clearly understood one another, but they persuaded themselves that this was so." At the outset Fénelon's letters show that he is suspicious, and still regards himself as a spiritual master who is to command; but at the close he is a submissive disciple. He follows the counsels of the seer of visions, repeating after her: It is necessary to become a little child (that is to say, *her* obedient child), to be guided by the "not seeing" and the "not knowing." He accepts, for the future, the subordinate part that Mme Guyon had ordained for him after one of her revelations: "*You shall be my tongue, you shall speak my very language, and together we shall accomplish all justice.*" The most absolute obedience is imposed upon him: "Your littleness must extend itself to the point of believing and practicing what God *causes to be said* to you by me" (*Letter* 108). "Acquiesce by *littleness* in that which I say to you, even if you should not yet know that I speak the truth to you" (*Letter* 75). Fénelon submitted to this oracle who declares herself infallible: "I am persuaded that God admonishes me by you, and gives me by you my daily bread. It is a state of complete infancy" (*Letter* 93). He puts his resolutions into bad verse:

> "I have a taste for *infancy*.
> With my rattle content,
> Weakness and *obedience*
> Of me a little child have made.
> Oh! Doctors, let me live
> Far from you, *from self afar*,
> Leave me, for I will follow
> The *blind law* of infancy" (p. 354).[5]

The lady makes this clever man share her belief in her revelations the more easily because she brings the most seductive promises. She assures him that a great providential mission awaits him. Fénelon will be "the general" of a great army of mystics, soldiers of St. Michael, or "Michelins," who will renew the world and establish the reign of true prayer.[6] God promised him, as He did

Abraham, that he should be the father of a great people: "God's designs upon you are great; you are the bright and shining lamp that will give light to the Church." As for Mme Guyon, she is to content herself, as she says, with remaining in the shadows, with being "the eternal victim, burning before God"!

For some time success seemed to confirm these fine predictions. Mme de Maintenon and a number of great ladies, notably the three duchesses, Colbert's daughters, doted on the doctrine of the *Moyen Cours* (the "middle course"); and Fénelon, the fashionable director, was admitted to expound these subtle novelties to the ladies of Saint-Cyr. This elite founded "*la Petite Église*" ("the Little Church"). Twenty-two years later (1711) hope rose to the point of exaltation. The prophetess had already announced that a child would aid in the triumph, and then she further explained that the Duke of Burgundy was referred to; he would become the chief of the Michelins. And so, when the grand-dauphin died, believers were persuaded that the throne was assured to Fénelon's pupil and that he would become his Richelieu. But the prince died a year later, and fortune returned no more to the Archbishop of Cambrai. Notwithstanding these successive deceptions, he never seems to have cured himself of his ingenuous hopes. This talented man, then, spent a great part of his activity in what was pure loss.

From this saddening story of the power of a woman, "half saint, half lunatic," we may derive a lesson for those who think that they can yield themselves up blindly to a visionary, and allow themselves to be guided by his or her revelations.

13. — The pretensions *of certain seers of visions.* They often decline to admit the need of any proofs other than their own personal conviction or the tone of piety prevailing in their revelations. At times even, in despair of otherwise vanquishing our blindness, as they call it, they bring us some fresh revelation that threatens us with the divine anger. But this one is no more proven than those that went before.

Finding myself exposed one day to this class of menace, I quietly replied: "Such words are a sign that your revelations are not from Heaven. The spirit who speaks to you does not know my interior dispositions. He is not aware that I *sincerely* wish to obey God, and that if I am exacting with regard to proofs it is *from a sense of duty*, in order to avoid illusions. God cannot threaten a man who acts from such motives; He ought to do so, on the contrary, if I committed the imprudence of believing you on your word alone. And, further, it is you that He should blame, for if I am without proofs, it is because you do not furnish me with that of sanctity."

The spirit responsible for the revelation (if there was one) felt that he had been unskillful. For in the next communication he took my side, declared that I was more than right, and that I was indeed a saint. He promised to supply, but *at a later date*, proofs that would be *irresistible*. I am still awaiting them; and yet the seer has left this world!

When a seer wishes to be believed on his bare word, we can generally get rid of him by saying: "You assure me that God speaks by your mouth. I have no right to believe you unless you prove it. What sign do you bring?" In his ingenuousness he has not expected this question, and retires abashed.

14. — Another example. I have heard of three persons living in our own time who have seen visions and who, each in her own Convent, had succeeded in getting her so-called revelations accepted without attempting to bring any valid proofs. People were simple enough to consult them about everything; so that they had practically taken over the management of their respective Houses. And thence arose disorders and indiscretions.

How ignorant one must be of true mysticism to be willing to consent to this form of government *by oracles* who tolerate no objections to their pronouncements!

15. — *Fifth rule*: to strive after **supernatural aims.** Let the director be occupied in working for his penitent's sanctification. Let him always come back to this question: What profit have you derived from the words that you think you have heard?

Even when he has not made up his mind regarding the nature of the revelations, he will thus, at least, have attained a very practical and important end; and in this way he remains on solid ground.

Seers of spurious visions are often not at all in sympathy with this kind of advice. They even end by going in search of another director, who shall be more credulous and less concerned about their sanctity. So much the better! We shall be spared much waste of time.

16. — *Sixth rule*: to avoid certain **dangers**. The *first* is that of **allowing oneself to be dominated** by another person. Let the director be on his guard against certain prophetesses who, dreaming of some great enterprise and seeing their own powerlessness, form the idea of **entering into partnership with their director**. They tell him that Heaven has chosen him; which is very flattering. They skilfully reserve the divine communications to themselves, as more in keeping, so they say, with the obscurity in which a woman should remain enshrouded; the priest will have the publicity of the exterior work, all the heavier tasks. In reality, they leave the priest the inferior position; *he has only to obey*. The visionary herself prefers to command, while protesting how greatly it distresses her to do so, explaining that it is not to her, but to God, that one is subject.[7] And, further, she often ends by compromising the priest in this way.

The suspicious thing here is not the fact that use is made of another person's prayers and actions; for many of the saints have felt the need of such a cooperation. It is the spirit of domination, the director being reduced to a state of servitude, his being asked to abdicate his reason in order to bow down before the authoritative revelations of another person, and this sometimes an ignorant one.

17. — *Second danger*. He must also beware lest the seer carry him away into sentimentality, into **romance**. There are persons who are tormented with the need of affection. Finding no outlet in the natural order, or not allowing themselves to seek for it there, they turn instinctively to the supernatural side. They dream of I know not what "unions of souls," declaring them to be inspired by God, while really they are merely ridiculous and *lead to nothing*. They claim to draw two souls mutually to the summits of divine love. But the end is often a human love; or, rather, from the beginning it was this earthly, violent, and blind tendency that sought so skilfully to satisfy itself. It concealed itself behind a mask; it was not recognizable. Let us mistrust all sentimentality, no matter what its pretext.

St. Bonaventure describes in very forcible language the danger of familiarities that had their rise in "charity and devotion" (*De profectu religiosorum*, Book II, ch. v; quoted also by Scaramelli, *Discernement*, No. 248). See also Blessed Angela of Foligno, ch. lxiv.

17 *bis*. — *Seventh rule*. To pray much and to make the person directed pray, in order to obtain the necessary illumination. God cannot fail to reveal the true way to those who ask it of Him humbly. If, on the contrary, we rely only on our natural prudence, we expose ourselves to being punished for our self-sufficiency.

---

2. *Seven rules for those who believe themselves to receive revelations and visions*

---

18. — In order to discern *the source* of these revelations, see the preceding chapter. Here are some other practical rules:

19. — *First rule.* Submit everything to a good **director** (see ch. xxvi [of *The Graces of Interior Prayer*]). St. Ignatius compares Satan to a seducer who wishes to keep his advances secret, and who loses courage if they are known (*Rules for the discernment of spirits*, I, 13). See also St. John of the Cross, on the necessity of overcoming a reluctance to disclose the state of the conscience (*Ascent of Mount Carmel*, Book II, ch. xxii).

St. Teresa, however, gives a direction allowing greater latitude in a case where it is a question of intellectual visions and not of revelations; and when, further, this way has been examined and approved, and nothing new occurs. "It would be as well at first to tell your case, under the seal of confession, to an extremely learned priest... or to some highly spiritual person.... When you have conferred with these persons, be at peace; trouble yourself no more about the matter, for sometimes... the demon gives rise to such immoderate scruples, that the soul cannot be satisfied with consulting her confessor only once on the subject" (*Interior Castle*, Sixth Mansion, ch. viii, 10, 11).

Eleven years before, in the Book of her *Life*, the saint would seem to give a contrary direction. But the contradiction is merely an apparent one. For it was then a question of interior locutions, that is to say, of revelations; and it was the time when, far from approving her new way, the learned were nearly all in accord in condemning it. "One of my confessors," says St. Teresa, "to whom I went in the beginning, advised me once, now that my spiritual state was known to be the work of God, to keep silence, and not speak of these things to anyone, on the ground that it was safer to keep these graces secret." Our Lord told the saint that she "had been ill-advised by that confessor," and that by acting thus she "might at any time fall into delusions" (*Life*, ch. xxvi, 5). See ch. xxvi [of *The Graces of Interior Prayer*], on directors.

20. — *Second rule.* To **mistrust revelations**, in general, and to remember that this way is very subject to illusions of the imagination or of the Devil. Even if the vision appears to be divine, to *mistrust the interpretation* that is given; to fear lest personal ideas should have *mingled* with it (see St. John of the Cross, *Ascent of Mount Carmel*, Book II, the end of ch. xxix).

21. — An **example** of wise distrust. Blessed Margaret of Ravenna and her companion, Blessed Gentilis (sixteenth century), had numerous revelations; but they protested that they attached no importance to them, and that credence must only be given to such things in them as were already known by means of the Church's teachings (for the first, see Bolland., January 23, First *Life*, No. 9; for the second, January 28, First *Life*, No. 16). And yet the Holy Spirit's action showed itself in them by predictions that were fulfilled, and by miracles.

22. — *Third rule.* **Not to ask or desire** this kind of grace,[8] and still for this reason, that it is very conducive to illusions. "No soul who does not deal with them [interior locutions] as with an enemy," says St. John of the Cross, "can possibly escape delusions in a greater or less degree in many of them" (*Ascent of Mount Carmel*, Book II, ch. xxx, p. 198).

23. — Some overly enthusiastic persons forget this rule when they are acquainted with an ecstatic (see Chapter Three, **31**) or anyone who is by way of receiving extraordinary lights at times. They are not satisfied with asking the assistance of their prayers, or with appealing to their human wisdom and experience, so as to obtain their advice. What they ask for are real revelations: "When you are in an ecstasy, *inquire* as to what will occur in this circumstance, or what decision I ought to come to." **These consultations are imprudent.** They expose the asker to erroneous replies, due to the imagination of the ecstatic.

Let us be content to express a desire to be enlightened from Heaven, and by the means that God selects. God alone can judge if a revelation is useful; if it is His good pleasure, He will make it. And, again, it must be accepted only at our own risk. The confidence placed in it may be greater if the seer has given many proofs that he is inspired by God.

It was in this way that numerous persons were able to make prudent inquiries of the Curé d'Ars. Long experience showed that his replies could be trusted. And then he was not asked bluntly for revelations, but for *direction*, which might be human to an extent that is hard to define.

It was thus also that in the seventeenth century St. John Eudes, Fr. de Condren, M. Olier, and the founders of Saint-Sulpice, sought after interviews with Marie Rousseau, a very holy woman, the widow of a Paris wine-merchant. "Although this poor woman," says M. Olier, "is of lowly birth, she is nevertheless the light and the councillor of the most illustrious Parisians by birth, and the most exalted in graces and virtues" (*Vie de M. Olier*, by M. Faillon, Vol. I, 4th ed., Part I, Book VIII, No. 17, p. 340). "I shall not describe the effect of her words. . . . When she is consulted, she replies in the simplest manner without explaining things, or enlarging on the exterior reasons which might serve to persuade people. She says simply: God wills that one should act in such a way. She has, sometimes, given advice contrary to that of the most enlightened persons, without being able to furnish any other explanation of the reasons of her replies, and *experience* has always shown that, after considering the matter well at their leisure, these persons found themselves obliged to return to her way of thinking" (*ibid.*, Book VIII, note 10, p. 369).

This last sentence shows that they tested Marie Rousseau's sayings instead of believing in them blindly; and, consequently, that they placed confidence in her only by degrees. M. Olier's biographer proves this, moreover, by facts (*ibid.*, Book X, No. 3, p. 438). Marie Rousseau herself was very reserved. Knowing prophetically that a group of priests were destined to found the work of the Great Seminaries and to reform the parish of Saint-Sulpice, she refused to associate herself with this enterprise for the space of ten years, although God urged it on her. Her resistance persisted until her director, Fr. Armand, S.J., made her give her consent in writing (*ibid.*, Book VII, No. 22, p. 302).

24. — *Fourth rule.* In the beginning, at any rate, gently to do our utmost to **repel the revelations** and to turn the thoughts away from them. (As to visions without revelations, see 5.) I say "gently"; for we must not go the lengths of causing a loss of the soul's peace and disturbing our prayer. If we cannot do more, we should keep this rule by inclining always in this direction.

I also say: "in the beginning, at any rate" (see an extract from St. Teresa, **36**, 1°); that is to say, as long as a prudent and learned director has not decided that a certain reliance may be placed in them. And it has been explained above (5) that he can show this confidence provisionally, without much delay, if these extraordinary facts aim *solely* at inciting the soul to the love of God, to mortification, and the other virtues. He will proceed more slowly if there are any instructions, predictions, and especially works that are difficult to achieve.

If prophetic visions occur from time to time, he may cease to repel them when it has been proved that they come exactly true and are free from other disadvantages. He must continue to be on his guard, however. Illusions are easy.

Even with these restrictions, the preceding rule may seem severe. It is, however, strongly enjoined by several saints, such as St. Ignatius (Bolland., July 31, Prelimin., No. 614), St. Philip Neri (Bolland., May 26, Second *Life*, No. 375), St. John of the Cross (*Ascent of Mount Carmel*, Book II, chs. xi, xvi, xvii, xxiv), St. Teresa (see Extracts), and St. Alphonsus Liguori (*Homo apost.*, Appendix I, No. 23). The principal reason is that which is predominant in the whole matter: the danger of illusion. "The Devil," says St. John of the Cross, "greatly rejoices when a soul seeks after revelations and *is ready to accept them*; for such conduct furnishes him with many opportunities of insinuating delusions and derogating from faith as much as he possibly can; for such a soul becomes rough and rude, and falls frequently into many temptations and unseemly habits" (*Ascent of Mount Carmel*, Book II, ch. xi, p. 95).

The saint adds two other reasons: the first, which, in reality, derives its value from the one that went before, is that "we are thereby delivered from the risk and labor of discerning between good and bad visions," which "is rather waste of time, an occasion of many imperfections and delay on the spiritual road" (*ibid.*, ch. xvii, p. 127). The contrary method "is not the way to direct a soul in matters which are of real importance, nor to relieve it of the vexation of trifles which are involved in particular apprehensions and perceptions..." (*ibid.*).

The other reason applies to communications that are not

purely intellectual, because "they are hindrances in the way of the spirit if they are not rejected; for the soul rests upon them, and does not regard the invisible" (*ibid.*, ch. xi, p. 92).[9]

St. John of the Cross is doubly severe when it is a question of visions or locutions affecting the bodily senses. "We must fly from them," he says, "without examining whether they be good or evil" (*ibid.*, Book II, ch. xi, p. 89).

When we strive in this way to repel a revelation, all that is implied is that we are not certain of its truth; we do not declare it to be false, or even partly so, and consequently there is no need to distress ourselves and to think that we have merited an illusion as a chastisement from Heaven. We must not take such a gloomy view of the situation. It merely resolves itself into a prudent precaution, without prejudging the rights and wrongs of the question.

25. — First objection. If the revelation comes from God, He will be angry if we repulse it. It is a want of respect.

26. — Reply. St. Philip Neri and St. John of the Cross affirm the contrary. This conduct is inspired, not by contempt, but by prudence (*ibid.*, ch. xi, regarding exterior visions). And, more than that, this refusal is a source of graces: "When the soul is resigned and not attached to such visions, the Devil retires, seeing that he cannot injure us then; and, on the other hand, God *multiplies His graces* in the humble and detached soul, placing it over many things.... The soul that is faithful amid these visitations God will not leave, till He shall raise it up, step by step, to the Divine union and transformation" (*ibid.*, pp. 93-94).

27. — Second objection. If we reject a vision, we deprive ourselves of the interior fruit that it should have brought us; and, further, when it orders us to perform an exterior work, the good that ought to result does not take place.

28. — Reply. As to the interior fruit, St. John of the Cross assures us that it will never be lost, for "all corporeal visions, emotions of the senses — the same is true of all other interior communications — if from God, effect their chief object at the moment of their presence, before the soul has time to deliberate whether it shall entertain or reject them." It is the same even with exterior visions, if they are from God. "Even if the soul wills it not, they produce their effects, chiefly and especially in the soul rather than in the body" (*ibid.*, p. 91, and chs. xvi, xvii).

If the object of the revelation is to instruct us, God has many other means by which to make His thoughts known to us.

29. — With regard to **external actions** that we are advised to perform by a revelation, when we say that the revelation itself is to be rejected, it is not suggested that these projects must be given up. It is enough that there should be other good reasons for undertaking them.

30. — There are merely **two precautions** to be taken: (*a*) to let ourselves be decided, at any rate chiefly, by the value of these reasons (4), and entirely so, if the revelation does not seem very certain; (*b*) to imitate St. Teresa (37), in not bringing forward the revelation as a reason to other people. In this way we shall avoid the temptation to take a tone of command, as though we were speaking in God's name. And, further, we thus augment our chances of success. For our hearers would be afraid lest we should first ask for their belief in the vision; they would very wisely require us to begin by justifying this claim, which is almost always impossible. Finally, the person who has had the vision will avoid a great source of trouble, namely, bitter or violent discussions, with those who dispute his inspiration; and objectors will always be numerous.

31. — Let us also note that the rejection of visions should not apply to those that are **deific** (*indéiques*), those of the Divinity. For these are merely a kind of mystic union. It is a question of *ex-deific* visions, those of created things. St. John of the Cross, although so rigid with regard to visions, notes this exception expressly: "This knowledge relates directly unto God, in the deepest sense of some of His Attributes... this becomes pure contemplation. . . . It is only a soul in union with God that is capable of this profound, loving knowledge, for *it is itself that union*... it is God Himself Who is then felt and tasted.... I do not say that the soul is to conduct itself negatively here, as in the case of the other apprehensions; because the Divine touches are a part of the Union to which I would direct the soul, and for attaining unto which I teach it to withdraw and detach itself from all besides" (*Ascent of Mount Carmel*, ch. xxvi, pp. 176-178).

32. — *Fifth rule.* If we believe a corporeal apparition of Our Lord or of the saints to be due to the Devil, not to go to the length of insulting it or **treating it with contempt**, any more than we should do towards a sacred picture that had been painted by a scoundrel (see Scaramelli, Tr. 4, Nos. 56, 68; and St. Teresa, *Book of Foundations*, ch. viii; *Interior Castle*, Sixth Mansion, ch. ix).

St. Philip Neri, however, held and followed the contrary doctrine (Bolland., May 26, Second *Life*, No. 374 and following). But on one of the two occasions when he ordered the person who saw the vision to spit in the apparition's face, he seems to have known by a revelation that it was a diabolic apparition. So the case is no longer the same as where there is a doubt.

33. — What is to be done **if the director orders** these contemptuous gestures? Here there are two opinions. According to the first, you must obey. For we should always do so where there is no sin; which is the case here, since in the intention of the seer of the vision the mark of contempt is not addressed to the saint or his likeness, but to the Devil, who is suspected of being present. St. Teresa submitted to her director in this way, and Our Lord said to her that she "did well to obey" (*Life*, ch. xxix, 7). The Blessed Virgin used the same language to Blessed Francis Ferrari, a disciple of St. Philip Neri.

In spite of the encouragement that she had received from Heaven, St. Teresa, at the end of her life, adopted the contrary opinion, namely, that it is permissible, and more seemly not to obey.

"My advice is, if you are given such an order, that, humbly alleging the reasons I have set before you, you should not carry it out" (*Interior Castle*, Sixth Mansion, ch. ix, 11).

34. — *Sixth rule.* If, in spite of yourself, you have visions, to be chiefly concerned in making them serve your **progress** *in virtue.* For if they come from God you will thus have attained the sole end that He desired. In the contrary case they cannot harm you.

St. Teresa says: "The good or the evil is not in the vision, but in him to whom it is given, and who does not profit by it in humility; for if he is humble, the vision, even if it came from Satan, *can do him no harm,* and if he is not humble *it will do him no good,* even if it comes from God" (*Book of Foundations*, ch. viii, p. 56).

The Ven. Louis du Pont relates that when Fr. Jean del Campo was in the novitiate, he received visions. One day, in anguish, he asked himself if he was not the sport of his own imagination. He then heard Our Savior address these words to him: "When you are hungry, if you are given a branch of a tree loaded with fruit, what do you do?" "I eat the fruit and cast the branch away," he replied. "Even so," Our Savior continued, "act in the same way with regard to the visions. Eat the fruits thereof — humility, patience, and the other virtues; and whatever the vision may be, be not troubled any more" (*Menology* of Aug. 11).

35. — *Seventh rule.* Display much calmness and **patience** if Superiors will not permit the execution of enterprises that you think have been inspired by Heaven or revealed. He who, in the face of opposition, is angry or discouraged, shows that he has small confidence in God's power and little conformity to His will; he will do well to attribute his want of success to these bad dispositions.

If God wills the project to succeed, He will be able to make the obstacles vanish suddenly at the time that He has appointed. This time is perhaps far distant; your scheme may even be realized only by your successors. What matter, provided that the good is achieved? You will, at least, have contributed to it by your efforts and your prayers, and your intentions will receive an eternal reward.

EXTRACTS
1. How we should do our utmost to ward off revelations, at any rate, at the outset.

36. — St. Teresa:

1° "There is need for caution... until it is certain from what spirit these things proceed. I maintain that, *in the beginning*, it is always *wiser to resist* these communications; if they come from God this is the best way to receive more of them, for they increase when discouraged" (*Interior Castle*, Sixth Mansion, ch. iii, 3).

2° "Nor have I heard where the earthly paradise is... as for asking His Majesty to reveal anything to me, that is what I have never done. In that case I should immediately think I was *imagining* things, and that I must be in a delusion of Satan" (Relation VIII, addressed to Fr. Rodrigo Alvarez, *Life*, pp. 463-464).

Regarding apparitions of Our Lord: "I most earnestly advise you, when you hear of God bestowing these graces on others, that you never *pray* nor *desire* to be led by this way yourself, though it may appear to you to be very good; indeed it ought to be highly esteemed and reverenced, yet no one should seek to go by it for several reasons" (*Interior Castle*, Sixth Mansion, ch. ix, 13).

Two notable reasons given by the saint are as follows:

(*a*) "Such a one is certain to be deceived, or at least is in great danger of delusion, for a door is thus left open to the Devil" (*ibid.*, 14).

(*b*) "When people strongly desire a thing, the imagination makes them *fancy they see or hear it*, just as when one's mind is set on a subject all day, one dreams of it at night" (*ibid.*, 15). And then to meet an objection, the saint adds: "Our Lord [by depriving us of these apparitions] does not deprive us of anything that can gain us more merit, for this rests in our own hands; thus there are many saints who never knew what it was to receive such favors, while others, who received them, are not saints at all" (*ibid.*, 19).

2. How we should regulate our actions not by revelations, but by sound reasons.

37. — St. Teresa:

1° Speaking of herself: "She *never undertook anything* merely because it came to her in prayer; on the contrary, when her confessors bade her do the reverse, she *did so* without being the least troubled thereat, and she always told them everything" (Relation VII, addressed to Fr. Rodrigo Alvarez, *Life*, p. 450).

2° Letter to Fr. Suarez, Provincial of the Society of Jesus, who had reproached the saint with having counselled a grave step on the strength of a revelation (February, 1578).

"Even supposing I myself had this revelation, which you call 'dreaming,' I could not be so imprudent as to wish him to make so important a change, *through any such cause...* for, thank God, I have many good friends who teach me what credit is to be given to such revelations" (St. Teresa's *Letters*, p. 115, 1902 ed.).

3° Speaking of locutions: "If they treat of some weighty matter in which we are called upon to act, or if they concern any third person, we should consult some confessor who is both *learned* and a servant of God before attempting or thinking of acting on them, *although we may feel more and more convinced of their truth and of their divine origin....* Our Lord will reassure our confessor, whom, when He so chooses, He will inspire with faith that these locutions are from the Holy Spirit. Unless He does so, we are under no further obligations in the matter. It would, I think, be very dangerous to act against our confessor's advice, and to prefer our own opinions in such a matter. Therefore, my sisters, I *admonish* you, in the name of Our Lord, never to do anything of the sort" (*Interior Castle*, Sixth Mansion, ch. iii, 18).

4° "When [however] they only *console* you, or *warn you of your faults,* it matters not from whom they come, or whether they are only fancy" (*ibid.,* 4).

38. — Fr. Balthasar Alvarez, speaking of consolations:

"It is not by these motions and consolations that a soul must regulate and direct itself, but by the doctrine of the Church... it would be a mistake to regard them as an *infallible* proof that God *wills this*, and does *not will that*.... They should consult enlightened directors, and confine themselves to what they prescribe" (*Life* by du Pont, Vol. II. ch. xxxiii, 3).

---

3. That the director should deal gently with those who believe themselves to have revelations.

---

39. — St. John of the Cross:
"But remember, though I say that these communications are to be set aside... it is not right for spiritual directors to show themselves severe in the matter, nor betray any *contempt* or *aversion*; lest their penitents should shrink within themselves, and be afraid to reveal their condition, and so fall into many inconveniences... rather, they must treat them with *gentleness* and *calm*, encouraging their penitents, and giving them every opportunity to explain them. And, if it be necessary, they must enjoin upon them this manifestation, for at times everything is necessary in the difficulty which penitents experience when they have to reveal their state" (*Ascent of Mount Carmel*, Book II, ch. xxii, p. 166).

40. — St. Teresa:
1° On the fear of being deceived in our prayer: "And certainly the affliction to be borne is great, and caution is necessary, particularly in the case of women — for our weakness is great — and *much evil may be the result* of telling them very distinctly that the Devil is busy with them.... Women should be directed with much discretion; their directors should encourage them, and bide the time when Our Lord will help them" (*Life*, ch. xxiii, 14, 15).
2° On supernatural locutions: "At times, indeed, very often this [voice] may be nothing but a fancy, especially with persons of

a lively imagination or who are afflicted with melancholy to any marked extent. I think no attention should be paid to such people when they say they see, hear, or learn anything supernaturally. *Do not disturb their minds* by telling them it comes from the Devil, *but listen to them* as if they were sick persons. Let the Prioress or confessor to whom they tell their story, *bid them think no more of it,* for such matters do not conduce to the service of God: the Devil has deceived many Christians thus, although perhaps it is not so in their case; therefore *they need not trouble themselves* about it. Thus we must accommodate ourselves to their humor; if we tell them their fancies *proceed from melancholia* [their nervous temperament, we should say], they *will never believe us,* but will persist in maintaining they have seen and heard these things, for so it seems to them. The truth is, care should be taken to keep such people from too much prayer, and to persuade them, as far as possible, to take no notice of their fancies" (*Interior Castle*, Sixth Mansion, ch. iii, 2, 3).

Notes

---

[1] Speaking of intellectual locutions, St. John of the Cross says: "The real and secure teaching on the subject is, *not to give heed to them,* however plausible they may be, but to be governed in all *by reason,* and by what the Church has taught and teaches us every day" (*Ascent of Mount Carmel*, Book II, ch. xxx, p. 198).

[2] Leo XIII said on this occasion that he often received letters of this nature, written, usually, by enthusiasts (*Vie*, by Mgr. de T'Serclaes, Vol. III).

[3] M. Maurice Masson, Professor at the Fribourg University, has published a very instructive book: *Fénelon et Mme Guyon* (Paris, Hachette, 1907). It is a collection of letters, covering a period of about a year (1689), at the beginning of the relations between the two correspondents. I summarize here the psychological study which this book furnishes; the facts are typical, and may serve for our instruction.

[4] See all the details of these fantasies in Maurice Masson's book pp. 4 and following.

[5] "J'ai le goût de *l'enfance*
De mon hochet content
La faiblesse et *l'obeissance*
De moi font un petit enfant.
Docteurs, laissez-moi vivre

Loin de vous, *loin de moi*;
Laissez-moi, car je veux suivre
De l'enfance *l'aveugle loi*."

6   Mme Guyon had decided the offices of this order. Besides the general, there would
be two assistants, a secretary, an almoner, a novice master, a *jailer*, a *street porter*, a
flower-woman, a portress, a female sacristan, a superintendent of recreations, and
other officers male and female, of less importance. In the midst of these fantasies
Mme Guyon retained sufficient practical sense to marry her daughter, aged thirteen, into the world of duchesses.

7   I have seen several examples of attempts of this nature. One of these persons assured me that I had a magnificent mission. Providence would take me to Jerusa-
lem, and there (with her aid, be it well understood) I was to bring the Jews throughout
the world back to the one true religion. What an attractive offer! To be charged
with the task of renewing the world and putting an end to all the conflicts of anti-
semitism! Only I had to resign myself for a long time to receive the divine commands solely through this new Egeria. In fact, I was *to begin by obeying*, and let myself
be led like a child; then later on, much later on, I was to receive my reward. It was
a fool's bargain. [Egeria was a 4th-century female pilgrim to the Holy Land.]
     Another that I was told of, had invented a "maternity of souls," which permitted
her to busy herself in all the trifling affairs of those whom she tenderly described as
her children. See above (**12**), the similar case of Mme Guyon.

8   Spiritualists have a diametrically opposite practice. If they invoke the souls of the
dead, it is in order to ask them for *information* or advice. However, their curiosity is
rarely satisfied. The replies generally teach nothing that was not already known, or
they make statements of unverifiable facts. Often, again, when it is a question of
difficult problems in science or philosophy, they are vague or contradictory. The
spirits (if it be that the medium alone is not responsible) have convenient ways of
escape; when they confine themselves to stating that these mysteries surpass our
human understanding, for example. This is a poor result.

9   "The soul can never attain to the height of the Divine union, so far as it is possible
in this life, through the medium of any forms or figures…. In the high estate of the
union of love, God does not communicate Himself to the soul under the disguise
of imaginary visions, similitudes or figures; neither is there place for such, but mouth
to mouth [as to Moses]; that is, it is in the pure and naked Essence of God, which is
as it were the mouth of God in love, that He communicates Himself to the pure
and naked essence of the soul, through the will which is the mouth of the soul in
the love of God.
     "The soul, therefore, that will ascend to this perfect union with God, must be
careful not to lean upon imaginary visions, forms, figures, and *particular intelligible
objects*: yea, rather they are an obstacle in the way, and *to be guarded against and
rejected*" (*ibid.*, ch. xvi, pp. 117, 118). "The objects of sense and the knowledge which
results from them are the occupations of a child. That soul which ever clings to these,
and which never detaches itself from them, will never cease to be a child… relying
in the outward veil of the senses which is childish, it will never attain to the Substance of the Spirit… These things the soul must not regard; yea, rather it must
renounce them wholly, having its eyes fixed on that spiritual good alone which they
effect… and we shall [in this way] also *pass by* that which He too would have passed
by, if we could without it have received the blessings He intends to confer, namely
the usage and appliance of sense" (*ibid.*, ch. xvii, pp. 126-128).

HISTORICAL AND BIOGRAPHICAL NOTES

St. Alphonsus Liguori (1696-1787). Italian moral theologian, founder of the Redemptorists, author of *The Glories of Mary* and many other works. His *Homo Apostolicus* (1759) is a short work on mysticism.

Eusebius Amort (1692-1775). German Jesuit philosopher and theologian. A very prolific writer, his *De revelationibus, visionibus et apparitionibus privatis regulae tutae ex Scriptura, Conciliis, Sanctis Patribus* (1744) deduced 125 rules for the discernment of spirits and was largely directed against Mary of Agreda's *Mystical City of God*. He continued the attack in his *Nova Demonstratio de falsitate revelationum* (1751).

Bl. Angela of Foligno (1248-1309). Italian third order Franciscan and visionary.

Anti-religious order laws. In 1901 the French government passed the Law of Associations, which required religious congregations to apply for legal authorization or be dissolved. Very few authorizations were granted, and 81 congregations of women and 54 congregations of men were disbanded.

Pope Benedict XIV (1675-1758). Prospero Lambertini, pope from 1740 to 1758. A distinguished scholar, his *De Servorum Dei Beatificatione et de Beatorum Canonizatione* is an important work on the processes of beatification and canonization.

Bizouard. Author of a 6-volume work, *Des rapports de l'homme avec le démon* (1863).

Bollandists. A group of Jesuits who, since the 17th century, have studied the lives of the saints. They are the publishers of the multi-volume *Acta Sanctorum* and *Analecta Bollandiana*.

Cardinal Giovanni Bona (1609-1674). General of the Cistercian Order and author of *Lapis Lydius* (1672), a work on the discernment of spirits.

St. Bridget (Birgitta) of Sweden (1303-1373). Foundress of the Brigittines and visionary. She was instrumental in persuading the Pope to return temporarily to Rome from Avignon in 1367.

Melchior Cano (1509-1560). Spanish Dominican theologian, author of *De locis theologicis*, on the sources of theology, published posthumously in 1563.

St. Catherine of Genoa (1447-1510). Widow and visionary, who cared for the sick in the hospital in Genoa.

St. Catherine of Siena (1347-1380). Third order Dominican and visionary. She was instrumental in persuading the Pope to return permanently to Rome from Avignon in 1376.

Comte de Chambord (1820-1883). Henri, Comte de Chambord, was the last claimant of the elder branch of the French Bourbon dynasty, the grandson of King Charles X. He spent much of his life in exile. After the Second Empire collapsed during the Franco-Prussian War, he lost his chance to become king because of his uncompromising ultraconservatism.

Commune of 1870 (sic.). Also called the Paris Commune. The revolutionary government that controlled Paris from March to May in 1871, during the Franco-Prussian War. Just before it was suppressed, it murdered the Archbishop of Paris as well as a number of priests and laypeople.

Anne Catherine Emmerich (1774-1824). German Augustinian nun, stigmatist, and visionary. Her visionary writings were published posthumously by Klemens Brentano. A cause exists for her beatification.

Lopez de Ezquerra. Priest, author of *Lucerna mystica* (1692).

François de Fénelon (1651-1715). Archbishop of Cambrai, France, author, and spiritual director. He came under the influence of Mme Guyon beginning in 1689.

Jean Gerson (1363-1429). Chancellor of the University of Paris and theologian, author of *De distinctione verarum visionum a falsis*, among many other works.

St. Gertrude the Great (1256-1302). German Benedictine nun and visionary.

Johann Joseph von Görres (1776-1848). German scholar, author of a 4-volume work, *Die Christliche Mystik* (1836-1842).

Cardinal Vincenzo Lodovico Gotti (1664-1742). Italian Dominican philosopher and theologian, author of *Theologia scholastico-dogmatica juxta mentem Divi Thomae Aquinatis ad usum discipulorum* (1727-1735), as well as a number of works against the Calvinists and Jansenists.

Jeanne Guyon (1648-1717). Quietist author and poet, who greatly influenced Fénelon.

St. Hildegard of Bingen (1098-1179). German Benedictine abbess and visionary. Besides her main work, *Scivias,* she wrote hymns, letters, books on medicine and natural history, etc.

St. Ignatius of Loyola (1491-1556). Spanish founder of the Jesuits, author of the *Spiritual Exercises.*

St. John of the Cross (1542-1591). Spanish doctor of mystical theology, co-founder (with St. Teresa of Avila) of the Discalced Carmelites. Author of *The Spiritual Canticle, The Dark Night of the Soul, The Living Flame of Love,* and *The Ascent of Mount Carmel.*

Marie Lataste (1822-1847). French visionary. She joined the Society of the Sacred Heart in 1844 and made her vows just before her death.

St. Lidwine (Lidwina, Lydwid, Lijdwine) of Schiedam (1380-1433). Dutch virgin and visionary.

Mary of Agreda (1602-1665). Spanish Discalced Franciscan nun and visionary. Her book, *The Mystical City of God,* has been controversial from its first publication.

St. Mechtild of Magdeburg (1240-1298). German Benedictine nun and visionary.

Melanie of La Salette, Secret of. In the years following the 1846 Marian apparition at La Salette, France, one of the visionaries, Melanie Mathieu-Calvat, published an apocalyptic prophecy which caused a great deal of controversy.

Miguel de Molinos (1640-1696). Spanish priest and founder of Quietism, a system of mysticism which advocated an exaggerated passivity towards God.

Karl Wilhelm Naundorff (?-1845). Pretender to the French throne, who claimed to be the Dauphin, Louis XVII. The real Louis XVII (1785-1795) died under obscure circumstances as a prisoner during the French Revolution. He was rumored to have escaped, and over the years some 40 people claimed to be the Dauphin.

Alvarez de Paz (1560-1620). Spanish Jesuit theologian and mystic, author of *De Inquisitione pacis sive de studio oratione* (1617).

Cardinal Jean-Baptiste-François Pitra (1812-1889). Outstanding French Benedictine scholar. He was an archaeologist, theologian, librarian of the Vatican, bishop, author, and editor. He edited the writings of St. Hildegard of Bingen (1882).

Jerome Ribet (1837-1909). French priest and mystical theologian, author of *La Mystique divine distinguée des contrefaçons diaboliques et des analogies humaines* (3 volumes, 1879-1883).

Saint-Médard Cemetery, events at. After the Jansenist deacon François de Paris died in 1727, a number of supposed cures took place at his tomb in the Saint-Médard Cemetery. This drew crowds of Jansenist fanatics of both sexes, who went into convulsions, screamed, and prophesied against the Pope. After the cemetery was closed in 1732, the convulsionaries continued their activities in private homes.

Duc de Saint-Simon (1675-1755). The *Memoirs* of Louis de Rouvroy, Duc de Saint-Simon, are an important historical source, especially for the last years of Louis XIV.

Giovanni Battista Scaramelli (1687-1752). Jesuit writer, preacher, and spiritual director, author of *Discernimento de' spiriti* (1753) and *Direttorio mistico* (1754).

Dominic Schram (1722-1797). German Benedictine theologian and canonist, author of *Institutiones theologiae mysticae* (2 volumes, 1774).

Hélène Smith. Pseudonym of a 19th-century Swiss medium, Catherine Elise Muller. She claimed to be a Hindu princess and Marie Antoinette in previous lives, and also to have the ability to be spiritually transported to Mars. She provided detailed descriptions of the Red Planet's people, civilization, language, etc. She was investigated by Theodore Flournoy, a professor of psychology who published his unfavorable findings in *From India to the Planet Mars: A Study of a Case of Somnambulism with Glossolalia* (English translation, 1900).

Francisco Suarez (1548-1617). Spanish Jesuit Scholastic theologian, author of *De Religione* and *De Oratione*, among many others. His *Collected Works* were published in 1630.

St. Teresa of Avila (1515-1582). Spanish doctor of mystical theology, co-founder (with St. John of the Cross) of the Discalced Carmelites. Author of *The Interior Castle, The Way of Perfection,* and *The Life* (autobiography).

Western Schism (1378-1417). The period during which there were two (and sometimes three) papal claimants, at Rome, Avignon, and Pisa. It was ended by the Council of Constance.